THE SLAVE SHIP
WANDERER

THE YACHT "WANDERER."

THE SLAVE SHIP
WANDERER

Tom Henderson Wells

UNIVERSITY OF GEORGIA PRESS
ATHENS

To My Son
PETER WILLIAM WELLS

Paperback edition, 2009
© 1967 by the University of Georgia Press
Athens, Georgia 30602
www.ugapress.org
Printed digitally in the United States of America

The Library of Congress has cataloged the
hardcover edition of this book as follows:
Library of Congress Cataloging-in-Publication Data

Wells, Tom Henderson, 1917–1971.
The slave ship Wanderer.
107 p. illus., map. 25 cm.
Includes bibliographical references.
1. Wanderer (Schooner) 2. Slave-trade—United States—History. 3. Slave ships. I. Title.
E449 .W47
380.1'44'0973   67-27139

Paperback ISBN-13: 978-0-8203-3457-8
ISBN-10: 0-8203-3457-X

Contents

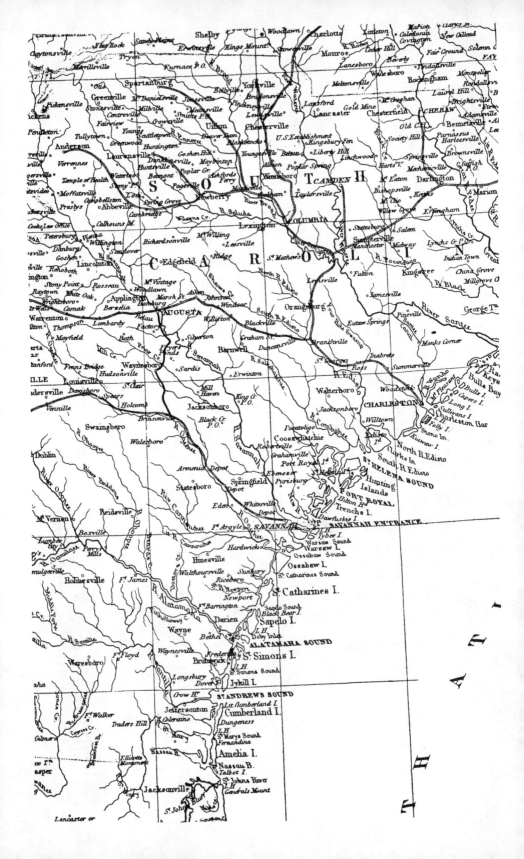

I

Charles Lamar's Savannah

FOR A QUARTER-CENTURY after American independence, Georgia was a frontier area, subject to depredations from Florida. Its agriculture was primitive and, except on the sea islands, not very profitable. Development of the cotton gin and of upland cotton brought the possibility of a money-producing staple crop to the area, but there were not laborers enough to handle the work.

Georgia had not had large-scale slave importations before state laws suspended and then national law forbade the overseas slave trade. For a time, surplus Negroes from worn-out plantations to the north flooded into Georgia, but thousands of these were syphoned off to booming states to the west.

Many men decided that laws forbidding introduction of African slaves were unjust to newly settled areas; a few, believing the laws unconstitutional or not legally enforceable, determined to violate them. On the south Georgia coast such a group of men challenged and defeated the United States government by landing and distributing more than four hundred African slaves in the only successful large-scale slaving expedition to this country after 1820. This landing from the yacht *Wanderer* took place 65 miles south of Savannah on one of the sea islands, but the center of activity was in Savannah.

About half these slaves were brought up the island-studded Savannah River a little later for distribution. Like the coastline, the river bank was lined with marshes and hummocks bearing groves of great, moss-hung live oaks. So flat was the countryside that a lookout in the tops of an inbound vessel at the Tybee Island

1

entrance could see the Exchange tower and the Lamars' new six-story rice mill 16 miles upstream. An incoming vessel would pass the giant, newly completed and as yet unmanned Fort Pulaski on Cockspur Island before entering the settled area around Savannah. In the lower end of town, close along the waterfront on the south bank, was the Lamars' newly built complex which included the rice mill, a cotton press, warehouses, and wharves. On upriver, still on the south bank, was the city's commercial center, the broad cobblestoned Bay. The Bay was a great outdoor warehouse and street, bustling with purposeful activity.

In the fall of the year it was piled high with thousands of cotton bales awaiting shipment to world markets. Along the waterfront were moored the cotton ships; most were small coastal schooners of 200 to 600 tons but some were square-riggers, the masts and yards forming a forest several ships wide along the full half mile of the Bay.

Back from the Bay, nestled among a dense growth of trees like rabbits peering through the grass, were some two thousand buildings, mostly dwellings, some lavish like those of the Lamars and Habershams, all with ramshackle quarters for the slaves who composed half of Savannah's 18,000 population. Every five blocks the streets opened to pretty parks which contained monuments to the city's heroes. Trees and graceful brick or shell paths gave this side of the town a leisurely look which contrasted sharply with the activity along the Bay. Over the entire area lay a constant dampness, and the stench of the swamps permeated the air. Roads out of town had to be covered with planks or shells to prevent carriages from miring.

The landward side of the Bay was lined with taverns wherever they could be crowded between commission houses and cotton buyers', ship chandlers' warehouses, sail lofts, the new Greek Revival Custom House, and the ancient city hall with its jail. Even in the daytime the Bay was no place for ladies, but the leading men of the town frequented the Exchange, the commission houses, and the Bay itself, for this was the commercial center of Savannah and all of Georgia. Cotton was king there and the Exchange was his throne room, with a small representation from the kingdom of rice. In the Exchange gentlemen in top hats and long black coats, piously intolerant of waterfront gambling, daily risked fortunes upon vague rumors that might cause the rise or fall of a fraction of a cent a pound in cotton during its long voyage to Europe.

Savannah was a city in transition. Its growth as a seaport had been restricted for almost seventy years by obstructions placed in the river during the American Revolution. Federal river clearance projects opened an eleven-foot channel by 1856 and subsequently dredged it to 20 feet. Increased sea-going traffic brought prosperity, new buildings, and added population. New streets, running in accordance with commercial needs, disrupted Oglethorpe's graceful but inefficient pattern. New industrial buildings were built between the old civic and commercial ones. The deepened channel also made direct commerce to Europe by deep draft vessels a civic and financial aim. Cornelius Vanderbilt of New York, George A. Trenholm of Charleston, and Charles A. L. Lamar of Savannah began plans for such a line.

Aside from making money, the men's principal interest was politics. Whigs, the largest political group, were losing ground. Political campaigns were violently fought and parliamentary law was an argument but not a rule in establishing a position. Loud voices, fisticuffs, and firearms were more effective and more widely used than logic or evidence. Court processes were spectator sports and outsiders often participated in proceedings. Savannah's James Wayne sat on the Supreme Court of the United States and on the local circuit court and did what he could to maintain decorum, but his voice and authority did not carry far outside the courtroom. The federal judge permanently in the area was John C. Nicoll, a quiet man who served as United States judge for the district of Georgia.

Nicoll's son-in-law was Charles Augustus Lafayette Lamar, who in 1858 became Savannah's best-known citizen when he was arrested for violation of slave-trade laws. Charles Lamar's background and personal wealth made him an unlikely slaver, but his operations in the case of the slave yacht *Wanderer* make him the central figure in this book.

A son of Gazaway Bugg Lamar, one of the richest and most enterprising men of the South, Charles Lamar was from the time of his baptism in the arms of Marquis de Lafayette in 1825 a public figure. Fiery, articulate, and opinionated, he was a controversial leader.

When he was fourteen years old Charles Lamar heroically tried to save his mother and five younger brothers and sisters when his father's steamship *Pulaski* blew up and sank off the North Carolina coast.[1] His Aunt Rebecca was his foster mother until Gazaway Lamar remarried a much younger woman, but Charles remained close to his father.

When Charles grew up he entered his father's vast enterprises, which included plantations, a commission house, a cotton press, ships, an insurance company, and shares in several banks, railroads, and other concerns. By 1846 Savannah proved too small for Gazaway Lamar's talents and ambitions. He moved to New York, leaving his Savannah interests in Charles's hands. Father and son conducted their businesses in such close co-ordination that one often drew upon the other for sums in the tens or even hundreds of thousands of dollars.[2]

Nevertheless, each had some activities quite separate from the other's. Charles Lamar was a partner in a Georgia gold mine with his friend Nelson Trowbridge, but he had nothing to do with his father's charity or religious activities, preferring the race track to church pews for investments. Like his father, he had the vision and the nerve to undertake the unusual and to see it through. For instance, the elder Lamar had assembled an iron steamship, the *John Randolph,* out of material prefabricated in Great Britain. Charles Lamar pioneered the introduction of South American guano for fertilizer and also set up a flour mill capable of satisfying the needs of Savannah and its surrounding territory.

Charles Lamar was not just an aggressive businessman. Like most Southerners of his day, he loved politics. He used to attend precinct or state conventions or local meetings, remaining quiet until at a crucial moment he would rush forward, gold-headed cane flashing, red beard thrust in the air, coarse voice demanding recognition. He was usually surrounded by supporters, and he did not require that they be social leaders. Charles Lamar was often the despair of genteel relations such as Mary Ann Lamar Cobb (wife of presidential aspirant Howell Cobb), John Basil Lamar (a great land-owner), Lucius Quintus Cincinnatus Lamar (U. S. senator, later Supreme Court justice), Mirabeau Bonaparte Lamar (former president of the Republic of Texas), and his sanctimonious father.

Nothing disturbed these people more than Charles Lamar's advocacy of reopening the African slave trade to the United States. The slave trade had every element that could fascinate him: abstract principle, twisted logic, general disapprobation, political machinations, high adventure, and quick, enormous profit. Charles Lamar was regularly a delegate at Southern commercial conventions where he enthusiastically supported Leonidas Spratt and William Gaulden in their strident efforts toward repeal of laws forbidding the African slave trade.

Lamar was a forceful advocate. When his father wrote that an expedition to the moon would be equally sensible and no more contrary to the laws of providence than a slave-trading one, Charles replied, "Did not the negroes all come originally from the coast of Africa? What is the difference between going to Africa and Virginia for negroes? And, if there is a difference is not that difference in favor of going to Africa?" He went on to write that if slavery was a positive good for slave and master alike, as Southern ministers and statesmen insisted, was not it desirable to bring as many Africans as possible into that blessed estate?[3]

Father and son were in harmony except in this matter. John B. Lamar wrote to his sister Mrs. Howell Cobb, "You remember our conversations about the Lamars & the prospect of some of them getting in the penitentiary. The way Charlie is going on I fear he will lead off in that way, if he escape a lunatic asylum."[4] Gazaway B. Lamar wrote to John B., "While on that score let me tell you that I am not on Charley's side in the controversy with Mr. Cobb— & I have repeatedly told him his errors—but he is so impulsive, & so crazy on that Negro question—that I can make no impression on him—."[5]

Charles Lamar was not content to wait for others to grant him a right he thought was already his. He was never interested in mere abstractions of right and wrong; if he had a "right," he intended to exercise it with vigor and profit. He was convinced that he had a right to bring in slaves and he proposed to do so. If forced to use round-about ways to secure his ends, he believed he could nonetheless avoid morally compromising himself because he considered the substance of his rights more important than bare theory.

When in July, 1857, he applied for clearance for his 273-ton bark *E. A. Rawlins* to go to Funchal, Madeira, off the west coast of Africa, he was refused, and the vessel was seized on suspicion of being a slaver. A search showed her cargo to include large quantities of pilot bread, rice, cowpeas, lumber, whiskey, and a number of firearms, all items that were typical supplies for slave trade but that might also be used for a normal commercial voyage. Lamar protested to the secretary of treasury and the *E. A. Rawlins* was released.[6]

She proceeded to Funchal where Captain A. Grant sold part of the cargo and spent $1,800 of the gold Lamar has entrusted to him, without going to Africa. He returned to this country by way of the West Indies and entered New Orleans instead of Savannah. Lamar thought Grant had been frightened away from the slave trade by the presence of English cruisers at Madeira.[7]

Lamar persisted. This time he divided responsibility. For captain he hired C. W. Gilly (or Gilley or Gilles). Supercargo was William Ross Postell, himself a capable mariner and a man of resolution and initiative. Postell was of a prominent South Carolina family, eight years an officer of the United States Navy, then commanding officer of two schooners in the navy of the Republic of Texas. Postell had resigned from the Texas navy in 1841 under a cloud of suspicion in spite of his reputation as an excellent captain and commanded small vessels out of Savannah. Postell was to be in charge of business affairs aboard the ship and was to be given two Negroes out of every hundred landed, plus $80.00 a month for the four months the *E. A. Rawlins* was expected to be gone.[8]

In early May, 1858, Captain Gilly brought the *E. A. Rawlins* to the port of St. Thomas, an island about four hundred miles northwest of the mouth of the Congo. While Gilly was ashore being refused clearance to depart, Postell and the mate, Eben Sears, ran off with the ship, stranding the captain and so angering Portuguese authorities that they threw Postell in jail when he came back in another ship a year later.[9] From St. Thomas the *E. A. Rawlins* probably went to the Congo. Along the Gulf coast United States Treasury officials were alerted to the possibility that she might land slaves there.[10] In August the United States consul general in Cuba wrote the secretary of state that it was rumored that the *E. A. Rawlins* had landed 658 Africans at Puerta de la Teja on Cuba's north coast.[11]

On July 31, 1858, the *E. A. Rawlins* got back to Savannah without papers under command of Postell; Sears had boarded the British bark *Penelope* at sea, her crew helpless from yellow fever, and had taken her to Charleston. The fact that in three months the *E. A. Rawlins* had left captains strewn over two hemispheres and had no clearance from her last port looked suspicious. She was seized by Savannah authorities. Her owner, surprisingly enough, was satisfied, and there was no evidence of misdeed, so she was released on December 11, 1858, and went to sea soon thereafter.[12]

At the same time as the *E. A. Rawlins* venture, Charles Lamar was bedeviling authorities with his vessel *Richard Cobden*. In May, 1858, Lamar's Charleston agent, Lafitte and Company, requested clearance for the *Richard Cobden* for the purpose of "taking on board African emigrants in accordance with the passenger laws and returning with the same to a port in the United States."[13] This was not as fantastic a scheme as it appears: both England and France countenanced such enterprises although both countries roundly condemned the slave trade. However, the collector at Charleston refused clearance.[14]

Lamar appealed to the secretary of treasury. Cobb replied that as no state of the Union would receive African Negroes as free men, it must be Lamar's intention to bring in slaves.[15] Lamar persisted; he would take his apprentices to Cuba. Cobb ruled that there was no distinction in American law between traffic in African apprentices and in slaves.

On July 5, 1858, Lamar published and distributed an 11-page pamphlet on the controversy. It is a strong and forceful presentation of the right of a ship-owner to send his property wherever he wished until such time as the government had evidence enough to make an arrest. He wrote, in part:

I am responsible only to the courts of justice; and you, as an officer of this Government, can only abridge me of that right upon the broad ground that the privileges of the citizens of this country are only to be enjoyed upon the sufferance of the executive. . . . [Do you claim] that rights may be withheld for fear of an abuse of them? That collectors may withhold a registry for fear the vessel may be turned to piracy? — the clearance, for fear she may return to smuggle? That the State Department may withhold commissions for fear the officer will violate his trust? That the executive shall withhold the halls and archives for fear the Legislators may do acts that will be detrimental to the public. . . .[16]

He did not get the clearance. The *Richard Cobden* made a voyage to England where she was involved in a collision and was forfeited for damages.[17]

The remonstrances of his father, the interference of the government, the objections by newspapers, and the unreliability of subordinates did not dissuade Charles Lamar from his purposes. He felt he knew his rights and he had tested the law enough to know its weaknesses. He would be more discreet, plan and organize better, and get better men and equipment. He and his ships, the *E. A. Rawlins* and the *Richard Cobden* were too well known; he would have to form a new expedition with some outside professional assistance. Accordingly, he established an informal clandestine company, bought the luxurious yacht *Wanderer,* prepared her for sea in a port where corruption was known to be widespread, and manned her with a suitable crew appropriately supervised by a trustworthy non-professional to prevent fraud. He would remain in the shadows of his great cotton press in Savannah, preparing for the distribution of slaves when they arrived in the United States.

II

Wanderer Embarks Slaves

IN THE TWENTY YEARS of her existence the schooner *Wanderer* was stranded, collided with, twice stolen, and twice condemned as a slaver. She acted as a pleasure craft, a slaver, a would-be pirate, a freighter, and a gunboat. She was reputed to have cost $25,000 to build, and even after eighteen years of abuse she sold for $6,000.

The *Wanderer* started her career in 1857, the plaything of Colonel John Johnson, a wealthy sportsman and member of the New York Yacht Club, who had spared no expense in making her one of the finest pleasure crafts in the world. She was built by Thomas B. Hawkins at the yard of Joseph Rowland in Setauket on Long Island. Her extreme hull form and rigging and the fineness of masts, spars, and sails made the *Wanderer* not only a thing of beauty but also made her breathtakingly fast. On numerous occasions she made 20 knots, far greater speed than her contemporary steamships and comparable to the great clippers. Even in light and head winds on one return trip to New York she averaged 7.5 knots for the nine days it took her to travel from New Orleans to New York. She had a long, sharp bow, a concave cross-section amidships (instead of the usual straight sides of the time), and a cutaway stern with only the rudder aft, rather than knuckles or bilging pieces found in most vessels of her time. Since the time the *Wanderer* was constructed, most sailing vessels have adopted similarly simple lines; today, seen close up, she would not seem as startling as she seemed in her own day.[1]

In January of 1858 Colonel Johnson was showing off his new

yacht on a trip to New Orleans. Stopping first for several days at Charleston where Johnson entertained many prominent people aboard his yacht, the *Wanderer* went on to Brunswick, Georgia, where she arrived January 20 with all her colors flying, just in time to enter her boat in the first annual regatta. The "Wanderer Jr" raced against four local boats and one from Charleston and won the 12-mile race by 300 yards. That night her officers attended the Regatta Ball. The mayor of Brunswick, Colonel Carey Styles, presented cups to the winners, and Colonel Johnson gave a speech of acceptance.[2] From Brunswick, the *Wanderer* sailed on to Key West and to New Orleans.

On the *Wanderer's* return to New York it was announced that she had been sold to William C. Corrie of Charleston, who, on Johnson's recommendation, was elected to membership in the New York Yacht Club.[3] Corrie immediately began collecting a group of adventurous friends to accompany him on a long cruise. The yacht was provisioned with the fanciest foods for the lavish entertaining Corrie enjoyed. But before Corrie could get to sea, the *Wanderer* was arrested as a suspected slaver.

In the 1850's New York City was the center of slave-trade activity in the United States. A modern study has identified twelve ships sold into the slave trade there in 1859 and ten in 1858.[4] Other vessels were manned or outfitted there, and several well-organized slave-trade companies are believed to have had their headquarters in New York. There are several reasons for New York's importance in the slave trade. It was a busy port with many legitimate sailings to Africa, which served to mask unlawful voyages. It had a large and fluid sailor population and an excess of medium-size sailing vessels whose cost had been lowered by the advent of speedy clippers and newly constructed steamers. Moreover, slaving equipment was easily available; a number of merchants had grown wealthy outfitting whalers and palm oil traders that were actually slave ships. But perhaps the most important reason was the character of United States Judge Samuel R. Betts of the southern district of New York.

Old Judge Betts was confident of his status as an expert on admiralty law. In other ports such as Boston and Key West, vessels had been condemned as slavers because they carried equipment and cargo usually found only on a ship on an illicit mission. By Boston or Key West reasoning, the presence of a large supply of water, rice, messing and cooking utensils, lumber, handcuffs, firearms, and money, or a majority of these items, was usually sufficient proof of intent to enter the slave trade. Betts consistently ruled that since these articles were not of themselves illegal and since it was possible for them all to be embarked in an ordinary vessel, a presumption of innocence followed unless corroborating evidence of guilty intention was produced. Many a guilty vessel was able to slip out of port when no such evidence could be found.[5]

Since slave-trade operations were common in New York, it is not surprising that when suspicious things went on in a shipyard, gossip would start. Because of her speed, the *Wanderer* had been in the public eye from the time of her construction. Upon being sold to Corrie, she was sent to a yard at Port Jefferson, halfway up the inshore side of Long Island. There tanks capable of holding 15,000 gallons of water were installed in her. At normal navy rations of the 1850's, a gallon a day per man for all purposes, this would allow the *Wanderer's* twelve-man crew and eight passengers 750 days at sea! It would allow 500 persons to go thirty days on navy rations or sixty days at half rations. Wealthy sportsmen would be expected to use a lot more water than sailors accustomed to severe water discipline, but the fresh water capacity was abnormally large for even a pleasure vessel.

When on June 8 the passengers, officers, and crew came aboard, they too created waterfront talk. One of the passengers was J. Egbert Farnum, an adventurer of the most violent nature. The crew was headed by Nicholas D. Brown, a swarthy, red-bearded Greek. The mate, William Brooks, was of similar character, and the men were a dark and hard-looking lot: Greeks, Spaniards, or Portuguese, singularly unsuited to form the crew of a vessel devoted to social amenities, but of nationalities and characteristics common in the slave trade.[6]

Not mentioned in the gossip was the fact that the *Wanderer's* first owner, John Johnson, usually said to be a New Yorker, was a native of Louisiana and the owner of a huge sugar plantation on the Mississippi River below New Orleans. The fast yacht he built was too large and carried too much sail to race under New York Yacht Club rules. He immediately displayed her in Southern ports, including New Orleans, Southern headquarters for the African slave trade to Cuba, in Charleston, which William Corrie claimed as home, and at Brunswick, Georgia, near where Charles Lamar had extensive land holdings and where his friend Carey Styles was mayor. All three of these men were importantly connected with the *Wanderer's* slave-trade expedition. Before she was a year old, Johnson was reported to have sold her for half her cost, although

Corrie, who never worried whether or not he told the truth, claimed to have paid $5,000 more than cost.[7]

The agent who handled the *Wanderer's* outfitting was Nelson Trowbridge. Had authorities thought to investigate his background, they might have found some interesting connections. In 1855 Trowbridge and Charles Lamar sold Cuban bonds. Trowbridge had handled the New Orleans part of the *E. A. Rawlins* affairs. Later, during the Civil War, Trowbridge was New York agent for Lamar's blockade-running concern.

It was in an atmosphere of curiosity and suspicion that the yacht's crew gathered at Port Jefferson. S. Norton, who as surveyor for the port supervised customs activities under the collector in New York, checked the *Wanderer's* papers and found them in order. Now, with almost all provisions aboard, the *Wanderer* needed only one more load of supplies, which Park and Tilford sent on the schooner *Charter Oak* on the morning of June 8. It had been Corrie's intention to pass to the north and east of Long Island rather than through the narrower and more crowded channel by New York City. When the *Charter Oak* arrived, there was extraordinarily low water in Port Jefferson. The additional weight of these supplies would give the yacht too great a draft to get across the bar, so, rather than load more stores in port, Corrie ordered the *Charter Oak* to an anchorage near New York, expecting to join her that afternoon. However, adverse winds held the *Wanderer* in port until the morning of June 9.

As she got underway a steam revenue cutter, the *Harriet Lane*, came darting out from behind a headland and hailed her; the *Wanderer* did not stop. But the wind was light and the steamer intercepted and forced the *Wanderer* to lay to. Deputy Marshal Maurice O'Keefe and one of the cutter's officers boarded and seized the *Wanderer* on suspicion of being fitted out for the slave trade.

Corrie was indignant; nonetheless, the cutter took the *Wanderer* in tow, added the *Charter Oak,* and anchored near the battery on the southern tip of Manhattan Island. The inspection of vessels and manifests was ordered for next day, and officers were stationed aboard the two suspected vessels.

Next morning the inspecting party had grown to include Assistant United States Attorney Theodore Dwight, United States Marshal Isaiah Rynders, as well as O'Keefe. When a reporter asked Marshal Rynders for permission to come aboard, O'Keefe bustled in before Rynders could answer and assured the reporter that there was nothing to see, that the *Wanderer* was too small, too costly, and too beautifully furnished to be used as a slaver. The reporter remarked that a single good cargo of illegal slaves would make enough profit to refurbish the yacht completely and that bulkheads could be removed in a few hours time to give additional space for slaves. O'Keefe would not let him aboard.

Less suspicious reporters wrote that while a heavy downpour interrupted the morning investigation, Corrie invited the officials to luncheon in his elegant cabin. There, in the splendor of Brussels carpets, flawless mirrors and engravings, rosewood furniture, tastefully selected books, and sumptuous food and wines, Corrie toasted, "If thine enemy hunger, give him food; if he thirst, give him drink." Everyone laughed at this good natured impudence, and the inspecting party soon departed. Nothing unwarranted had been found. There were vast quantities of fine hams, cheeses, tinned meat and fish, excellent wines, and enough similar items for eight months' cruising at full rations for the passengers and crew embarked.

There were no handcuffs, no huge cooking pots, no lumber for extra decks, no large supplies of rice and beans, and above all, no clear-cut evidence that wrong-doing was contemplated. The *Wanderer* was released on order from United States Attorney Dwight. And now comes another curious part: Corrie had said his vessel was completely ready for sea, but after the inspection she hung around New York for about a week before she left for Charleston.[8]

The inspection appeared to have been an honest and thorough one and there was no public or newspaper demurral at the time, although the incident had wide publicity in both Northern and Southern newspapers. After the *Wanderer* became notorious the *New York Herald* reported a rumor: "R's [Rynders'?] mouth was sealed with plasters intended for the shin, and English and Yankees were bamboozled with better liquor than they were used to. The most business man the old Commodore [Corrie] met on his travels, was R. Says the old Commodore, 'I just pulled out my book and paid him — real business Yankee.' "[9]

On June 25 the *Wanderer* sailed into a Charleston which was seething as usual with controversy and defiance. The *Wanderer's* mission was a subject in the current discussions. In May a commercial convention for Southerners had been held in Montgomery, Alabama, and Charleston's Leonidas Spratt had introduced a series of resolutions to reopen the African slave trade to the United States. The convention had debated and then tabled the resolutions and Spratt had returned home to push for legislative action in

South Carolina. The *Charleston Mercury* opposed consideration of the measure on the grounds that it was divisive when the South needed unity. The argument had continued during the *Wanderer's* detention in New York. Hot-headed Charlestonians fired a salute as the *Wanderer* entered their harbor.[10] Unnoticed amid the hubbub of dinners, parties, and Corrie's extravagant entertaining, supplies were bought from Hugh Vincent, chandler and owner of the slaver *Jehossee,* and slaving gear was got aboard: items such as 30 six-quart pans, 20 five-quart pans, 50 one-pint tin cups, wooden spoons, and 12,000 gallons of water.[11]

When Corrie came to Acting British Consul J. Pinckney Walker and asked for British protection for himself and his traveling guests, Walker saw no reason for refusing them: "Corrie was a member of the New York Yacht Club which entitled him to some consideration," he said later. Walker issued protections for Corrie, Farnum, two persons named Brent and Beman, plus Nicholas Brown under the name of Dennis. Walker had known Corrie a long time but did not attend Corrie's social gatherings.[12]

Before leaving port on July 3, 1858, Corrie told Charlestonians he wished to inspect the estate of a deceased uncle at Port of Spain, Trinidad. This made a convenient excuse for heading in the direction of Africa. Upon his arrival on this isolated British possession, he quickly ingratiated himself with the authorities. He entertained and was entertained by the governor and members of his family. Again covering his movements with convenient papers to account for the direction he was heading, he let it be known that he wanted to visit Napoleon's tomb on St. Helena, but suddenly and without being properly cleared, the *Wanderer* left Trinidad. Her log for July 27 states: "En route Trinidad to St. Helena." She headed southeast in the general direction of the lonely island, but she never got within 900 miles of it. She bucked easterly winds for fifty-one days, and the first land sighted was Cape Padrone Bon on the south bank of the Congo River, the center of the slave trade. The next day, September 16, 1858, she entered the river.[13]

Each year in September slave-trading activities fell off because fevers sickened the crews of vessels on the coast. This September a French man-of-war lost twenty five men in two weeks from fever. Nevertheless, Corrie and his friends explored the wild, beautiful African scenery, wearing their yacht club uniforms, called on native chiefs in their palaces to observe their customs, and with open-handed hospitality entertained all the white inhabitants of the outposts visited.[14]

Up the Congo River lay the British steamer-of-war *Medusa*
keeping watch on two American vessels in the river, the *Kate Ellen*
and the *Rufus Soule*. J. Egbert Farnum brought back to the United
States the story that the officers of the *Wanderer* hoodwinked the
British officers, who never suspected the *Wanderer's* reason for
being there. Farnum reported that at a dinner party aboard the
Wanderer he invited the captain of the *Medusa* to inspect the
Wanderer to see if she was a slaver, at which all the disbelieving
and highly entertained British officers roared with laughter.[15]
Farnum's story has been believed for a hundred years because
most people have thought that the British seized American ships
they strongly suspected of being slavers. But the truth is that although the *Medusa's* officers suspected the real nature of the *Wanderer*, heard the hammering as the extra deck for slaves was laid,
and reported so to the Admiralty,[16] they did not seize the yacht.

The British let the *Kate Ellen* go, also. However, they did seize
the *Rufus Soule*, whose captain admitted his guilt. Some Americans thought that the capture of the *Rufus Soule* was merely a
gesture by the British since they let the captain and crew go free
to re-enter the slave trade. These Americans thought that the aim
of the British officers and men was winning prize money for cap-
tures, not suppressing the slave trade.[17]

Americans had little confidence in the endeavors of the United
States Navy. The *Wanderer* remained either in or near the Congo
River for almost a month before she was seen by a single American
warship. Readers of the *New York Herald* would know that Flag
Officer Thomas Conover was notified of the *Wanderer's* presence
within nine days of her arrival, and he had two ships at his immediate disposal in St. Paul Loanda, about two hundred miles south
of the Congo; yet he waited two weeks before he got his first vessel
underway.[18] He sent the *Vincennes*, which by any standard was
the worst vessel in his command, and he failed to send even that
sorry craft directly to the Congo River where both the *Wanderer*
and the *Kate Ellen* were.[19]

When the *Vincennes* arrived in the Congo River, instead of
making a captive of either slaver, Captain Totten got into an
argument with the captain of the British steamer-of-war *Viper*.[20]
Belatedly, Flag Officer Conover got his flagship *Cumberland* underway and had her pursue a leisurely voyage up the coast to the
mouth of the Congo, where he made a futile show of forming an
expedition of small boats which rowed up the river and asked the
captain of the *Medusa* if he had any word of the *Wanderer*. The

reply was that the *Wanderer* had left the coast some days before with over 350 captives.[21]

Newspaper readers could say that two incompetent navies had again been fooled by the slavers. Few saw that an American foreign policy that proclaimed freedom of the seas was providing a refuge for slavers.

III

The African Squadron Fails

THE WEBSTER-ASHBURTON Treaty was supposed to provide for co-operation between American and British African squadrons, and, to a large measure, it did. The United States, having a small navy, little money, and no bases in the area, always had trouble in maintaining her required eighty guns on the African coast. Commanders complained that their vessels were too slow, too large, or that steamers were needed. Unfortunately for the suppression of the slave trade, United States policy and the tendency of outstanding officers to avoid unhealthful and monotonous duty made the African squadron the backwater of the navy. The few new or fast ships and the better officers were employed elsewhere. Storeships to supply the African squadron were few and always late. Coal, even for cookstoves, was so scarce that steamers were not used. At the time of the *Wanderer's* cruise, the largest United States fleet yet assembled, except in the Mexican War, was gathering for a show of force against Paraguay; even the *Harriet Lane* was going. Another year went by before the first United States steamer-of-war arrived off Africa.

It requires the equivalent of about three ships in commission to keep one ship on station: one is being fitted out, manned, dispatched, or it is returning, repairing, or paying off; the second is operating; the third is keeping the operating ship supplied.

Since it took almost two months for a ship to arrive on the African station, and since little food was available on the African coast, replenishment was a big problem. Small ships could carry only about two months' provisions; even the *Cumberland* had to

16

load stores about every three months. Since the storeship could be detained only a short time and since there were no rapid means of communication, the commander had to set up a rendezvous between his ships and the storeship months in advance. The storeship was a sailing vessel, usually fat, sluggish, and old, and she was frequently delayed by weather. The result was that much time was spent in waiting at the rendezvous, even though the big flagship usually took the stores for one or more of the smaller vessels still on patrol.

Many different schemes for increasing the effectiveness of the squadron were tried, but a depressingly large proportion of the time—perhaps 70 per cent of the vessel's time in African waters—was spent on logistics, on administration, and on recuperation from periodic ravages of fever.

The British offered the American squadron the use of their nearby bases, but the secretary of the navy refused to use them and also refused to allow establishment on shore of coaling stations or permanent bake ovens. The reason for his reluctance to set up overseas bases was that creation of a base could reduce the fleet's flexibility. As convenient as a base might seem, it needed support, and the support might exceed the value of the base. In addition, British-American tension demanded that American warships not be made in any way dependent upon British bases.

It would not be making too many excuses for the American and British squadrons' failure to capture the *Wanderer* to bear in mind that during 1862, when most Southern ports were in Confederate hands and the Federal blockading fleet consisted of over 250 relatively modern vessels patroling a coastline approximately the same length as the African slave coast, two out of every three blockade runners succeeded in getting through. There were but five United States sailing warships and about eighteen British sailing and steamships guarding the African coast.

But the size and efficiency of the patroling squadrons were not the only problem; the slavers had their own well-developed defenses. After a slave ship made contact with a dealer ashore in Africa, there was a wait while the cargo was assembled. Depending upon the state of the trade, the prices offered (usually about fifteen or twenty dollars each), and the type slaves desired, as long as six weeks might pass before delivery could be made, during which time the slavers would be highly vulnerable to discovery and seizure. Traders stationed lookouts up and down the coast, and naval officers were convinced that they kept spies among the crews of the patroling warships. By whatever means they achieved it, traders usually had knowledge of the whereabouts and prospective movements of naval vessels. Thus a slave ship might be told to be off a certain point of land forty days after initial contact, showing a black flag at the forward part of the vessel. If all were clear, a similar flag would be shown ashore; if not, then a different signal would be given and the ship should return in another week.[1] Furthermore, during the *Wanderer's* operations the French government was recruiting and bringing off indentured Africans for employment in that country's tropical colonies, a thinly veiled servitude which meant that the barracoons were filled and emptied of Negroes who might be diverted to regular slavers with little trouble.[2]

When the *Wanderer* encountered the *Medusa* up the Congo River, the British warship was at anchor in a strategic location to interfere with the loading of slaves aboard the American vessels *Kate Ellen* and *Rufus Soule,* which were awaiting an opportunity to sneak slaves aboard. Within a few weeks the captain of H.M.S. *Viper* burned the *Rufus Soule.* The reasons that the freedom of the seas had apparently been violated were understood by Flag Officer Thomas Conover but not by Commander Benjamin J. Totten of the *Vincennes* or by newspapers in the United States. The crux of the situation was the difference between American and British slave trade laws. The act of May 15, 1820, of the American Congress made the captain and crew of a United States flag vessel suspected of involvement in the slave trade liable for arrest under charges of piracy; if they were found guilty, their execution was mandatory. On the other hand, an act of the British Parliament authorized the officers of British war vessels to board, seize, and destroy without trial ships engaged in the slave trade and unable to prove their nationality; British law did not regard slave trade as piracy.

Complicating the problem, some British naval officers still regarded Americans as intruders on Britannia's oceans and arrogantly and high-handedly insulted United States merchantmen and interfered with their lawful trade. The United States denied that foreign ships had the right to stop and search American vessels and had fought the War of 1812 over this question. Many veterans of that war, including Conover, were still on active duty. To the American mind, it did not matter that American ships in African waters were seldom legitimate traders; the trouble with accepting visit and search in one part of the world was that it became a right anywhere. The American government agreed that a British warship might possibly be justified in boarding a merchantman to ascertain her nationality, but it insisted that no American vessel could be searched by a foreigner. Hence slavers flew the American flag, carried American papers whenever possible, and usually managed to evade capture by the inadequate African squadron maintained by the United States.

Exasperated British naval officers therefore devised a scheme by which they could do some damage to the slave trade without offending American public opinion. They would board a suspected slaver and, if they were fairly sure that she contained slaves or slaving equipment, would threaten to detain the ship and her crew until an American man-of-war, expected at any moment, arrived. The American warship would search, seize, and take back to the United States the offending ship. A piracy trial would follow in the United States, and sooner or later someone would get hanged.

Most captains took the easy way out and destroyed evidence of American nationality, thereby allowing the British to scuttle an ownerless derelict; in this way slavers lost their ships but not their lives. The captain of the *Rufus Soule* had taken this alternative, but the *Kate Ellen* stuck by her flag and refused to open hatches. Even though the *Medusa's* boarding party smelled the slaves below closed hatches, the captain refused to give up his American identification, and the *Medusa's* captain let the *Kate Ellen* go rather than become involved in a freedom-of-the-seas case.[3]

For ten days the *Wanderer* stayed in the Congo River laying a slave deck and making preliminary arrangements for a cargo of slaves. During this period she was frequently visited by British officers from H.M.S. *Medusa,* who suspected that the *Wanderer* would become a slaver at first opportunity.[4]

In a report to the British Admiralty, Commodore Charles Wise told of the activities of the *Rufus Soule,* which he believed were similar to the *Wanderer's* operation. The *Rufus Soule,* wearing American colors and carrying American papers, entered the Congo and sent word to slave traders in the interior that a cargo was wanted. A few days later the slaver was offshore in sight of high ground. There the slave dealer burned three fires which formed corners of a great triangle and then flashed lights to indicate how many hundred slaves he had. The slave ship signaled back, using colored lights whose meaning Commodore Wise was unable to determine. He believed they indicated the time and location for pick-up.[5]

For September 26, 1858, the entry in the *Wanderer's* log reads:

"Got underway [from the Congo] and proceeded to sea. Gave the Sch. *Margrate* a trial and passed her like the wind." Two pages are then missing and the first whole sheet following begins with the statement: "These two pages have been torn out on account of the upsetting of the ink stand on them. W V B [William V. Brooks?]." The log then continues in the same handwriting until October 4 when it reads, "at 10 A M arrived at Benguela after 8 days hard beating against the wind and current." There are no further entries, although many blank pages remain.[6] Inasmuch as the *Wanderer* loaded her cargo of slaves sometime between October 11 and 17, it seems odd that the mutilated section should occur for a period three weeks earlier. The previous portion of the log is free of erasures and contains few corrections.

It is a kind of family joke among mariners (but serious business among sea lawyers) that something always happens to the log on the very page in which a collision, grounding, or other mishap is recorded. In the case of the *Wanderer,* offending pages that might have included the happenings of three or four days are missing. What could have happened between September 26 and 30 that W V B or someone else aboard the *Wanderer* wanted to conceal? And why did this mutilated record survive? The *Wanderer* probably carried at least one other log book; it was common practice for slavers to carry near duplicate records of various kinds for presentation to searching authorities.

The most probable reason for ripped-out pages would be an incriminating statement written in the log by the boarding officer of a British man-of-war. Many British officers were so outraged by the frustration of their efforts to capture American slavers that it was common practice for such officials to enter unsubstantiated, derogatory, or even insulting material in merchant ship logs. Once slaves were on board they would serve as evidence in the event of an encounter with an American man-of-war, but such a note could be inconvenient if American naval officers boarded the *Wanderer* while she was awaiting embarkation of her slave cargo. It would cause a meticulous inspection to be held. If it was not a boarding remark that had to be removed, the offending pages may have inadvertently recorded self-incriminatory information such as signals made, accomplices met, or rendezvous kept.

In either case, reproduction in the new log book of all the entries since June plus happenings and weather data during the interim would therefore be necessary, but the maintenance of parallel logs would take several days. Once the new log was completed the need for the original log passed and it should have been destroyed. Why was it not? Again one must guess. Perhaps it was merely overlooked. Perhaps a member of the conspiracy wanted a little leverage for later blackmail against his confederates or protection from them. It is known that J. Egbert Farnum offered a log of the *Wanderer* as part of his deal in turning state's evidence for his freedom.

From October 4 until the *Vincennes* made a vain pursuit on October 18, the *Wanderer* is unaccounted for. In two weeks the *Wanderer* might have gone to and returned from any port within a distance of a thousand miles. Wherever she was, she was up to no good, for during this time she crowded a cargo of almost five hundred human beings into her tiny hold. Probably these people were embarked between the Congo and Benguela, forty miles south—the *Wanderer* was sighted and chased by the *Vincennes* in that vicinity. Commodore Wise told the Admiralty that unlike other slave vessels, which loaded in the Congo River, the *Wanderer* loaded her slaves offshore.

The *Vincennes* was the oldest and least efficient of Flag Officer Thomas Conover's five-ship African squadron and was commanded by Commander Benjamin Totten, his worst captain. Totten was author of a Naval Academy textbook on seamanship but had a service reputation as a timid sailor and a tyrant. Even worse, perhaps, than Totten's inefficiency and tyranny in operating his own ship was his contentiousness toward the British, for the effectiveness of the American African squadron was largely dependent upon co-operation with the large, experienced British naval squadron in those waters.

Flag Officer Conover's flagship, the frigate *Cumberland,* was at Loanda, in present Angola, when the merchant bark *Sea View* came in, nine days from the Congo. She reported that the *Wanderer* and the brig *Helen (Kate Ellen)* were there when she left on September 15.[7] The *Vincennes* entered Loanda next day in accordance with her orders, but Conover did not issue his new cruising orders for two weeks, during which time the sailors passed the hours, as they frequently do now, making knives out of scrap metal. Abolitionist circles held that Conover did not want to take a slaver. This is not consistent with his correspondence or his reputation, nor is it borne out by presently known correspondence between his British counterpart and the British Admiralty. However, he was old and weary and inefficient. The *Wanderer* was not yet the notorious vessel that she became after the autumn cruise in 1858. Moreover, estimates placed the numbers of American vessels annually engaged in the African slave trade to Cuba or Brazil at seventy or more. Hence, Conover probably felt he had to think in terms of his total responsibility and act in accordance with well-matured designs and not dash off in a disorganized way after one or two ships. He made a good, if tardy, plan, and it almost worked.

Conover ordered the *Vincennes* from Loanda north to Ambriz, 70 miles south of the Congo, thence up the coast, touching at every slave mart and commercial place, searching carefully for American vessels in the slave trade, "examining closely the Congo River and its immediate neighborhood and by cruising backwards and forwards, striving to deceive the slave dealers and to elude the vigilance of their spies and agents."[8]

On October 14 the *Vincennes* arrived at Kabenda, twenty-five miles north of the Congo's mouth, where she fell in with H.M.S. *Viper,* whose captain told Totten's lieutenant (Totten was ill) that officers of H.M. Steamer *Medusa* had a day or two before boarded the *Kate Ellen* with slaves embarked but had released her because she was flying the American flag and had American papers. He did not mention the capture and burning of the *Rufus Soule.* Captain Totten found out about the *Soule* on October 16 when stranded American crew members came out to complain of an outrage to the American flag. The *Viper* had left port. Totten headed down the coast looking for the *Cumberland* so he could report the incident to his superior.[9]

Thus he encountered the *Wanderer* just as the schooner came darting out from the beach. The *Vincennes* tried to intercept, but the best she could do was 8½ knots, whereas the slaver was making a good 20 without even using her gaff topsails and flying jib.[10] With a strong breeze from astern and a thousand miles of open water before she would encounter the doldrums there was probably not a ship in the world, steamer or sailing vessel, that could have overtaken her. On October 23 Captain Totten discovered that he had been pursuing the *Wanderer;* by that time he was so deeply involved in argument with the captain of the *Viper* that the escape of the *Wanderer* probably seemed relatively unimportant.

The *Cumberland* arrived off the mouth of the Congo River shortly after the *Vincennes* had left, having missed her at sea. Since the *Cumberland* drew too much water to enter the Congo, Conover sent a boat expedition up the river under the *Cumberland's* energetic and ambitious captain, Commander John S. Missroom, who received reports from H.M.S. *Medusa* that the *Wanderer* with slaves aboard had outrun the *Vincennes*.[11] Conover could hope that the *Dale* or the *Bainbridge* cruising to the west might happen in the path of the *Wanderer* and catch her unawares, but this chance, slim at best, came to nothing. The *Wanderer's* voyage to the United States was unopposed from the time she outraced the *Vincennes*.

IV

Slaves Are Landed

IT TOOK THE *Wanderer* only about six weeks to reach Jekyll Island. A more suitable spot for her purpose can hardly be imagined. Like the other Georgia sea islands, Jekyll lay a few miles off the mainland separated from it by a marsh of cattails, eel grass, wild rice, and a channel three or four feet deep. The eastward side of the island had beautiful sandy beaches whose shallow gradients and rolling surf made them fearful places to approach in small boats and impossible to approach in larger vessels. Jekyll's only safe landings were where Jekyll Creek or Dubignon Creek cut through the marshes. Screening the island from passing craft were great oaks heavily festooned with Spanish moss. A lovelier, lonelier, more melancholy spot can scarcely be conceived.

Unlike most of the sea islands, Jekyll belonged to a single family, the Dubignons. Christophe Dubignon, a French royalist, bought it during the French Revolution and built himself a sturdy house of tabby (shell concrete). In 1858 the island was owned by John and Henry Dubignon and their sister, Mrs. Robert Hazelhurst, wife of a Brunswick physician. John Dubignon managed the place and in November, 1858, was the only white person living there; even the overseer had recently been discharged. Only a week before the *Wanderer's* arrival the following advertisement appeared in the *Savannah Daily Morning News:*

(Adv) Notice

All Persons are warned against landing on the Island of Jekyl,[1] for the purpose of gunning, cutting wood, removing wrecks, or in any way trespassing on said island. Suits will be immediately commenced against any

24

one found on shore with guns in the possession. Captains of coastal vessels will pay particular attention.

John DuBignon
Henry DuBignon, Jr.[2]

Dubignon slaves raised sea island cotton, corn, and foodstuffs on a long, narrow clearing which ran diagonally across the upper part of the island through the oak trees. Sometimes six weeks would pass before it would become necessary to send a boat to communicate with the steamboat that passed the northern end of the island en route to or from Brunswick, the nearest port. Jekyll was isolated, but it was handy to such navigable rivers as the Altamaha, Turtle, Satilla, and Little Satilla. St. Johns in the new state of Florida was 25 miles south. Savannah lay 65 miles north, an overnight journey.

By the time the *Wanderer* arrived near her destination food, water, and slaves' health were likely to be at low levels. Shipping lanes off Georgia were so concentrated that a chance sighting might occur at any time, and if authorities were alerted, law enforcement agents would form a network through which it would be hard to land slaves or to escape after landing them. The *Wanderer* had to make an immediate landing.

The low, featureless country afforded few landmarks to help a navigator unfamiliar with those waters. Constantly shifting sand bars demanded the up-to-date and detailed knowledge of a local pilot. The *Wanderer* made her landfall on Cumberland lighthouse, two miles across St. Andrew Sound from Jekyll Island. It appears probable that she timed her arrival to be offshore before dawn in order to make a night signal for a pilot and to have a full day to offload the Africans. No pilot answered her signal. She probably stood on and off shore hoping her pilot would come out. No pilot came. With few exceptions the remainder of the conspiracy was so meticulously worked out and the secret so carefully kept that one can be sure that a pilot had been selected and instructed but was not available when needed. Yet the ship had to discharge her cargo at once.

About sunset on November 28, Corrie and William Brooks left the yacht outside the bar and rowed a small boat through choppy St. Andrew Sound in to the beach inshore of the lighthouse. There they found Horatio Harris, substitute lighthouse keeper. Corrie introduced himself as Cole or Cook and his companion as Brookson and asked for a pilot to Jekyll Island. He said that they had come to bring off some gentlemen visiting the island. The two looked ragged and unkempt for yachtsmen; yet it often happened in those days that a sailing vessel could be becalmed for a week or storm-tossed for days and become low on water or provisions. Since there had been rough weather for several days, Harris thought little of their appearance until Corrie said they were from the *Wanderer*. Harris knew that yacht. He had been aboard her the year before when she visited Brunswick. Rumors about her being in the slave trade were widespread along the coast. The *Savannah Daily Morning News* had even reported her en route to the Gulf with a slave cargo on September 21, several weeks before she picked up the Negroes. The name *Wanderer* must have meant "Slaver" to Harris. He had no particular feeling about the slave trade, but he knew there was money and excitement connected to it. He said that the regular lighthouse keeper, James Clubb, was a retired pilot and was over at Jekyll Island on a visit. Maybe he would bring the *Wanderer* in. Harris did not much want to go to Jekyll Island that night, but he was dying of curiosity. He agreed to take Corrie and Brooks to Clubb. On the way over, Harris began to ask questions.

"Is she carrying slaves?"

"No," replied Corrie. "I am sorry that she is not. I would like to land forty thousand."

A little later he admitted that she was carrying slaves but quickly changed this to indentured apprentices from Africa. He mentioned his own and Brooks's real name and told Harris a little about the voyage, but Harris forgot what was said when interrogated in court.[3]

It was only a short pull across the sound and up Jekyll Creek (two hours of back-breaking labor being a short pull in those days) to the landing and then a half-hour stumble through the dark to find James Clubb. Clubb said he was at Jekyll Island Light when he first met Corrie and Brooks. This light does not appear on any known official list; presumably it was a private beacon maintained by the Dubignons. At any rate, John Dubignon was present when the meeting took place. At first Clubb did not want to have midnight dealings with the *Wanderer,* but Corrie pled with all the earnestness of truth that his vessel was in distress, that he was about out of food and water, and he begged Clubb to bring him in that night. As an act of mercy, Clubb agreed to bring the *Wanderer* in at first light of dawn. On second thought he saw it "was a money-making piece of business and thought he had a right to come in for a share." He demanded $500 for the piloting job, which usually would have brought only $15 to $19. Later, at the Dubignon house the Dubignons and Nelson Trowbridge had an argument over

Clubb's demands, and the Dubignons said they would pay Clubb. They signed a note in lieu of cash.[4] It was clearly extortion, and Clubb did not even stay bought; he turned state's evidence as soon as a little pressure was put on him and immunity was offered.

Clubb did a good job as a pilot. In the darkness between five and six on the morning of November 29 Clubb boarded the *Wanderer* and brought her across the bar in the teeth of a southwesterly breeze and up through St. Andrew Sound to an anchorage about 200 yards off the Dubignon landing. Clubb, like all good pilots, was not easily distracted by unusual sights aboard his ship, but as it grew light he could see forty to fifty filthy Negroes lying on the afterdeck. They appeared listless and emaciated but showed no signs of maltreatment or restraint. They were a weird looking lot; most had their teeth filed, some carried tribal tattooes on forehead or chest. Several had peculiarly shaped heads or jaws. Though the temperature was in the sixties, most were entirely naked. Some wore shirts, trousers, or wrapped themselves in blankets provided by the yacht.[5]

The Dubignon's big yawl boat assisted the *Wanderer's* two boats in landing the Negroes under the supervision of Nicholas Brown and some Spanish-speaking men, including sailors named Arguivi and Rajesta. Clubb and Brooks stood on the beach watching the landing with two Englishmen who had been on the yacht. Harris hung around gawking. When asked in court about the *Wanderer's* crew, Harris said that he was so amused and excited by the sight of four hundred naked Negroes that he had not noticed the white men at all. Among the cargo were only a few grown men and women. Most were boys twelve to eighteen years old. After disembarking they squatted or lay around campfires speaking an unintelligible tongue which contained some Spanish or Portuguese words.

After the blacks were ashore Clubb took the *Wanderer* to Little Satilla River and anchored her two miles upstream where she could not be seen by passing ships. From the hold where hundreds of Negroes had lain on temporary decks too close together to permit them to stand erect and without any sanitary facilities at all there rose an unbearable stench. The yacht was alive with cockroaches but appeared in good shape except for being weatherbeaten and having some sails damaged. The crew began cleaning her.

The blacks were turned over to two Dubignon Negroes, Polydore and Jack, both of whom had been brought from Africa in their

youth. A camp was set up. Dr. Hazelhurst found most of the new-
comers suffering from nothing worse than diarrhea, dietary defi-
ciencies, and skin diseases. None died in his care.[6]

The slaves having been landed and the yacht hidden, Brown
was rowed down Jekyll Creek shortly after midnight and, calling
himself Mr. Wilson, caught the steamer *St. Johns,* Captain Nicholas
King, as she passed on her regular run from Florida to Savannah.
In Savannah Brown notified Charles Lamar of the *Wanderer's* arrival. By midnight of December 1, Lamar, Trowbridge, John F.
Tucker, and Brown, now known as Dennis, were aboard the steam
tug *Lamar* on their way to Jekyll Island.

The *Lamar,* one of the first iron steamers built in the United
States, constructed by Gazaway B. Lamar but sold several years
previously, was usually employed in bringing ocean-going vessels
up the river to Savannah. This time she had a longer cruise, her
first to Jekyll Island that anyone could remember. Captain Luke
Christie was in Claghorn and Cunningham's store at about eight
or nine that evening when Captain Stevenson, the agent for the
Tow Boat Company, entered and told him that his steamer had
been employed to go below but Christie would not be needed as
the parties chartering her had their own captain, whom Christie
understood to be Captain Henry J. Dickerson. For some reason
Dickerson declined to go at the last minute, and they had to take
Christie. This increased the number of people who knew about
the enterprise, but the Negroes had to be dispersed as soon as
possible. It was given out that the *Lamar* was headed for Fernan-
dina, Florida, for a load of cedar.[7]

On December 2 the *Lamar* stopped at Brunswick to pick up
Thomas Bourke, brother-in-law of the Dubignons. Off the north
end of Jekyll Island Henry Dubignon came out in a boat and
showed Christie where to anchor. Brown and four Spanish-speaking
men embarked about half the Negroes on the *Lamar,* and by nightfall she was underway with Lamar, Tucker, and Brown aboard.
Threading her way through the coastal islands during daylight and
passing Savannah under cover of darkness, the *Lamar* reached an
anchorage 16 miles above Savannah on the South Carolina side
that was pointed out to Captain Christie by Tucker. Under Brown's
supervision the Negroes, one of whom was dead, were put off at
John Montmollin's plantation.[8] Tucker's Blakely Plantation lay just
across the Georgia side of the river.[9]

The next day, December 7, Brown, Rajesta, and Arguivi made
their way downriver to Savannah where they took a room in the

well-known City Hotel to wait a few days for departure of the next ship for New York. In the meantime the *Lamar* began a second trip to Brunswick.[10]

About December 12 or 13 Captain Hillary B. Frazier of the *Augusta* was ordered by his agent to embark approximately 170 Negroes a few miles upriver from Savannah on the South Carolina side. Frazier was not told exactly where to pick them up, but as he got opposite Mr. Potter's place six miles from Savannah a boat put out from shore with some white men aboard who showed Frazier where to get his cargo, about ten more miles up river. These slaves were from the group brought to Montmollin's plantation ten days before in the *Lamar*. After the Negroes were embarked under another white man, Frazier dropped downriver and let the guides off where he first saw them. On the way back toward Augusta the white man fed his charges. About two miles below Augusta and half a mile below Horse Creek on the South Carolina side the Negroes were landed in a wood yard. The white man gave Frazier a Negro boy for his trouble. Frazier returned to Augusta with his new possession. He kept the boy in his house for a few days, but so many people came to see him that Frazier found his African a nuisance and returned him to the donor.[11]

From the wood yard the Negroes were taken to the Tillman plantation near Hamburg in the Edgefield section of South Carolina, and to the plantation of Robert L. Butler who acted for Thomas and Robert Lamar, cousins of Charles. This area was a principal slave-trading center for the Southeast and utilization of it would facilitate further distribution.

The Negroes not sent up the Savannah River were quietly distributed from the Jekyll Island area. During the next few months newspapers contained a steady flow of reported sightings of *Wanderer* Negroes in various parts of the South.

In some way, possibly in the *E. A. Rawlins* which sailed from Savannah about December 13, the crew of the *Wanderer* and the two Englishmen were whisked out of sight. Captain Farnum got to Charleston in time to catch the New York boat on December 12. When Corrie paid Captain G. W. Stockwell, a Brunswick pilot, $100 to bring the *Wanderer* up to Brunswick where she arrived December 5, the only persons aboard were Horatio Harris, whom Corrie had hired as shipkeeper, and an unidentified lame man.[12]

In the first weeks after the landing there were comments from many sources to the effect that the *Wanderer* was not large enough to have brought more than about eighty slaves from Africa and that she had most likely been used as a decoy for some large vessel lurking off the coast of the United States. But it would not have been practical for the *Wanderer* to operate with a slower vessel. The critical time when underway was the approach to the coast, when speed and maneuverability were needed. To insure that sailing ships would be at a preselected place out of sight of land at an appointed time in the nineteenth century (or twentieth century before radio and radar, for that matter) called for an accuracy in navigation and luck in weather entirely out of the realm of probability. To have one vessel hover about a rendezvous waiting for the other would be to invite capture.

Hugh M. Davenport of the collector's office in Savannah estimated the space aboard the *Wanderer* in which Negroes could be stowed at about 2,550 square feet with the slave deck installed. He said that the usual rule of thumb was sixteen square feet per passenger, giving her a capacity of only 115.[13] An old British regulation was five slaves for every three tons displacement, making a theoretical slave capacity of about 380. If the Negroes were stowed closely, "spoon fashion," as it was called, each could have occupied as little as five or six square feet, especially as most were young boys. The *Echo,* captured only a few months before off Cuba with 330 slaves aboard of an original 470 embarked, was only 92 feet long (compared with the *Wanderer's* 104 feet) with a beam of 22 feet (compared with the *Wanderer's* 26.5).[14] The *Wanderer's* 15,000-gallon fresh-water capacity would have allowed about two-thirds of a gallon of water per day per man for a crew of 12 and a slave cargo of 487 for a cruise of approximately 45 days.

How many Negroes were actually loaded aboard the *Wanderer* in Africa?

George Cheever, custodian of the material found aboard the *Wanderer* when she was seized in December, 1858, testified that one of the notebooks kept in Corrie's handwriting contained the penciled entry, "On deck, 17th—came to anchor. List of passengers, 487." This notebook never was introduced in evidence, probably being among the items delivered to Charles Lamar when he bought the *Wanderer* at auction on April 16, 1859.[15] Horatio Harris' testimony that both Corrie and W. V. Brooks told him that they had left Africa with 490 is consistent with Cheever's statement.[16]

British consuls in Charleston (Bunch) and in Savannah (Molyneux) gave the numbers 471 and 400, respectively, in reports from unknown sources submitted to their government shortly after the landing.[17] The commander of the British African squadron estimated that space was available for 600. A correspondent from the *Vincennes* sent the *New York Herald* a letter from Loanda within ten days of the *Wanderer's* sailing, setting the figure at 350.[18] He was apparently repeating waterfront gossip which neither his captain nor Flag Officer Conover reported to seniors.

The *Savannah Republican* reported the existence of a paper marked "List of Cargo, 10 to the Talie" which indicated a total of 409 Negroes. The *Republican* believed this to represent the number embarked in Africa, but it surely referred to the number landed.[19] In the first place, there would be little reason for saving an old memorandum sheet from Africa, since the slaves were purchased for cash. Secondly, the dispute over numbers landed, as well as the vastly increased value of each Negro after landing, would make both sides retain their landing tally sheets. Also, considering that one body was jettisoned on the way in, there was a discrepancy of only three between the 413 Corrie had admitted to Clubb when he agreed to pilot the yacht and the 409 of the tally sheet. The figure of 409 is also consistent with Brooks's statement to Clubb that they had lost sixty, seventy, or eighty Negroes en route, out of the 490 he said were embarked. For these reasons, 409 appears to be the best estimate for the number landed on Jekyll Island.

Other estimates made within a short time of the landing were 400 (United States Attorney report to Solicitor General), 320 (Molyneux, from unknown sources), and 350 (*Savannah Republican,* which doubted that the *Wanderer* could have carried so many on a long voyage). The *Augusta Dispatch,* obviously the victim of propaganda, said, "We learn on good authority that the original cargo consisted of 420, and that not one of them died or was seriously ill on the passage."[20]

V

The Government Seeks Evidence

AS SOON AS THE *Wanderer's* slaves were disembarked, her crew thoroughly scrubbed the vessel inside and out, removed feeding equipment, and dismantled the temporary slave deck (but overlooked its fittings) in order to eliminate the tell-tale marks of the slave trade. Corrie went ashore to see Collector Woodford Mabry, who was responsible for the ports of Brunswick and Darien. He told Mabry his yacht entered St. Andrew Sound to take shelter from a storm. Giving a cursory look at the papers, none at the ship, and accepting Corrie's statement that the St. Helena seal was missing because the United States consul there was on leave, Mabry gave Corrie clearance for his vessel to proceed to Charleston on December 5.[1]

Soon Darien was seething with reports that a vessel had landed Africans, that groups of strange Negroes were traveling up the rivers, and that unfamiliar steamers were making night runs among the coastal islands. Woodford Mabry began to worry about the clearance he gave Captain Corrie. Closer examination of the *Wanderer's* papers disclosed a second irregularity: her clearance from Trinidad lacked a consular seal. Guessing that the *Wanderer* was the rumored slaver, Mabry hired a boat, inspected the yacht (which he found clean, shipshape, and well appointed), made inquiries about her recent activities, and then canceled her clearance. On December 8 he communicated his suspicions to United States Attorney Joseph Ganahl of Savannah and asked for instructions. He did not report his conjectures to John Boston, the collector in Savannah, or to the secretary of the treasury, but Ganahl kept

Washington, D. C., authorities informed and saw to the Savannah area himself.

After Mabry's letter was sent to Ganahl, the *Lamar* came to take the *Wanderer* in tow to Savannah. Mabry was thoroughly alarmed. Backed by local citizens, he refused to allow the *Wanderer* to leave Brunswick until he got instructions from Ganahl. At this Captain Corrie abandoned his vessel so fast that charts, letters, personal belongings, his trunk, and papers all remained aboard.[2]

Ganahl received Mabry's letter on December 11, 1858. He had already heard rumors of a landing of slaves somewhere down the coast. Now he started action. Casting about town he soon learned that three untidy looking strangers wearing coarse seamen's clothes had checked in at the City Hotel about 3:00 P.M. on December 7 shortly after the Florida boat came in. Their trunk followed them a little later.[3]

There might have been a fourth man at first, according to Michael Cass, the hotel clerk, but only three, Nicholas Dennis Brown, Miguel Arguivi, and Juan Bt. Rajesta, signed the register. Only Brown spoke English. There seemed to be some question as to whether the others knew how to spell the names they wrote in the register. The two Latins insisted on calling Brown "Captain," although he objected to the title. When the clerk asked if they had come from New Orleans Brown said they had. All three were dirty, unshaven, and had the weary, unkempt appearance of men just in from a long voyage. They stayed in their room until dusk, then went to William O. Price's clothing store and bought complete outfits of fancy clothing for $200 in gold. Price, who made a hobby of other people's business, asked a lot of questions but got few answers. When Brown finally admitted that he had been in New York, Price—who had also heard rumors of a landing of Negroes down the coast—asked if he know Mr. Miller (a well-known slaver) there. "What, Jack Miller?" was Brown's reply. This convinced Price that he was talking to a slaver, as did a Spanish laundry mark in a watch pocket of Brown's trousers.[4]

With no more to go on than the fact that the three ill-clad strangers had a lot of money and two of them spoke Spanish, Joseph Ganahl took Marshal Daniel Stewart to the City Hotel and arrested them on a piracy charge only half an hour before they were to catch a boat for New York. Ganahl told Brown that he was in the gravest of difficulties and had better call upon his friends for help. Brown replied that he was a stranger in town and knew no one, but within a few minutes John Owens, Savannah's most distinguished criminal lawyer and C. A. L. Lamar's personal attorney, was at the jail trying to arrange bail. The remarkable promptness of Owens' arrival was the link Ganahl had so far between the *Wanderer* and Charles Lamar. Ganahl informed Owens that the three were charged with piracy under the act of May 15, 1820, and that they would be confined in the Chatham County jail.

Ganahl reported the circumstances to the solicitor of the Treasury on December 15, 1858, and proceeded with speed, vigor, and courage to uncover as much evidence as he possibly could. He was operating in a community filled with rumors, but it was apparent that William Price would be his only co-operative witness. Other men might be made to testify, but there would be no more voluntary informers. Ganahl subpoenaed not only men known or rumored to have information but also all those living or working along the watercourses, including plantation owners, overseers, doctors, pilots, and steamboat captains.[5] In a letter to Mabry carried by Deputy Marshal Adrian La Roche, Ganahl suggested subpoenas for Lamar, Trowbridge, Tucker, the Dubignons, Clubb, and Harris. He also subpoenaed such prominent planters as J. S. Montmollin and R. L. Butler. He obviously intended to overlook no one who might be involved in the venture or have knowledge of it.[6]

The first step in the legal processes was arraignment before the United States commissioner. If he found adequate cause for investigation, a United States grand jury could indict possible offenders for criminal trial before the United States circuit court for piracy cases or United States district court for lesser felony cases. The yacht could be tried by a United States circuit or district judge sitting as an admiralty court and following special admiralty procedure. Approximately forty witnesses were called before Commissioner Charles Henry the week before Christmas.

Ganahl got Collector Boston to send the Revenue cutter *James C. Dobbins,* Captain Robert Day, to Brunswick to seize the *Wanderer.* Ganahl established that neither the United States consul nor the vice consul had left St. Helena in months. Thus Corrie's statement that he had been unable to have the *Wanderer's* papers endorsed there was false. It was plain that the *Wanderer* had never been to the island.[7]

While law enforcement agents tried hard to secure *Wanderer* Africans as evidence, Lamar and his associates tried just as hard and with more success to conceal their prizes, and when a Negro was seized they used every possible legal device, trick, or even force to recover a captive. An African from the *Wanderer* was an absolute necessity to any successful prosecution and both sides knew it.

While the subpoenas were being served Genahl had Marshal Daniel Stewart send his assistants out in search of evidence. Deputy Adrian B. La Roche left Savannah for Brunswick on December 17 to take possession of the *Wanderer* from Collector Mabry. He seized books, charts, log, and Corrie's abandoned trunkful of personal belongings. Marking and delivering these items to Mabry for safekeeping, he turned the *Wanderer* over to Captain Day, who brought the yacht in to Savannah on December 21, 1858, while La Roche went by way of Jekyll Island with instructions to arrest any Africans he could find. Although he sloshed about the swampy island all day he found none.[8]

Deputy Edwin Gordon was sent directly to Jekyll Island to serve a subpoena on John Dubignon and to arrest African Negroes. He was accompanied by his friend Mr. Blount, who had no official position, and by a pilot who stayed with the boat. As Gordon and Blount came up the path which the pilot said led to the Dubignon house they came upon a group of Negroes dancing around a fire. They got within three hundred yards before the Negroes ran and hid in the brush, Blount in hot pursuit. Gordon found one old American Negro named Sam who said he belonged to Dr. Hazelhurst and was alone in that place.

Just then Henry Dubignon rode up and demanded to know what Gordon was doing on his island. Gordon showed his warrant. Dubignon said his brother was not there, but he turned and rode off toward the house. Meantime Blount had found one Negro boy in a hut and momentarily had caught another who got away. Gordon was now in a dilemma. He could leave Blount with the captive while he went after John Dubignon, but Blount had not been deputized and might lose possession of the prisoner. Gordon decided to hold the bird in hand, embarked his party in the small boat, and went back to Brunswick to catch the steamboat for Savannah.

Captain Freeborn of the *St. Mary's* refused to let Gordon and his captive sail from Brunswick without proper clearance. Gordon thought that Freeborn was unduly strict, that a deputy should be able to move the boy to the adjacent customs district without clearance. Woodford Mabry had authority to clear a slave and was said to be on board, but Gordon was unable to find him before Mabry left the steamer. Gordon had to disembark his evidence and drive him up to Savannah in a buggy.

Gordon and his charge (Blount had disappeared) arrived in Savannah on Christmas Eve, and the boy was placed in the police barracks. On Christmas Day he was turned over to Marshal Daniel Stewart. Stewart thought the little fellow looked too sick to stay in jail, so he took him to George Wylly's establishment, apparently a combination slave hostel and hospital which Wylly maintained for his own large holdings and as a commercial place.[9] Some five hundred visitors came to Wylly's showroom to see the wild African boy.

The *Daily Morning News* editor was among those who observed the Negro. He reported the captive to be a happy, cheerful boy of about twelve or fourteen years, with an extraordinary gift of mimicry and an ability to repeat exactly words of any language spoken to him, though without understanding them. Later reports said that a substitute stood in occasionally to enable the real African to get some rest. Still later reports said that the whole show was a hoax, that what spectators had seen was a Sea Island Negro born of Santo Dominican slaves resident on that island and not an African at all.[10]

In the evening Wylly turned the keys over to his slave caretaker, Simon, as was his custom, and went home. About eleven o'clock Christmas night Simon was awakened by someone rapping at the door. Sticking his head out his upstairs window, he saw two white men and a Negro with a bundle on his head. One of the men called that he wanted to put his servant up for the night. Simon came down and unlocked and opened the door only to feel the muzzle of a pistol in his ear. If he made a sound, he was told, he would have his brains blown out. Where was that African? Simon went up and got him. The men threw the African some clothes which he put on, and they left together. The boy was not seen again.[11]

In Macon about midnight of December 27-28, Deputy Marshal Thomas L. Ross was walking along the platform in the depot smoking a cigar while waiting to board a train being prepared to leave for Albany. Just as he swung into the smoking car he heard a man say, "There's a couple of greenies in there." Ross saw two wild-looking Negro men the center of attention but without escort of any kind. As he got closer he could hear them talking in some outlandish tongue or repeating perfectly words or phrases in any language their tormenters tried. When someone said, "You are a couple of damned fools," they delighted the onlookers by repeating this. Their teeth were filed and one man had tattoos on his forehead. When Ross examined this tattoo the other motioned that he had one on his chest.

Ross asked around to find who was responsible for the blacks. Nobody claimed them; one person in the crowd guessed they were *Wanderer* Negroes. The express agent, John Smith, was looking after them. Ross herded the Africans off the train. Smith demanded a receipt. Ross told him to go about his business and took the two, later identified as Gumbo and Cuffee or Black Hawk, into custody. The city jailer was at the circus and could not be found, so Ross locked his captives up elsewhere for the night. He then telegraphed both Stewart and John Boston that he would deliver his men the next day. A heavily armed escort of ten men came to meet them outside Savannah. The captives were placed in the county jail where they stayed, caring for the jailer's horse, cleaning the yard, and working in the garden. They were first-rate evidence in the coming trials of the *Wanderer's* owner, captain, and crew.[12]

On December 16, 1858, before it could have reached the solicitor's hands officially, United States senators could read in the New York and Washington newspapers an almost verbatim copy of Genahl's report of his and Mabry's actions concerning the *Wanderer*.[13] That day the Senate passed a resolution asking President Buchanan to communicate any information he might have "if not incompatible with the public interest — in relation to the landing of the barque *Wanderer* on the coast of Georgia with a cargo of Africans." The President did not reply until January 11 and then merely stated that it was a fact that slaves had been landed and that the government and local authorities were aggressively trying to discover and bring to justice those involved.[14] The truth was that the man on the street in Washington had as much information about the *Wanderer* as had been received officially by the attorney general or the solicitor of the treasury.

The mention of these two officials brings up one of the chief difficulties in enforcing the laws against the African slave trade: the lack of clear-cut responsibility by one government agency. General measures were up to the Department of the Interior. The solicitor, as head legal authority in the Treasury Department, supervised collectors of customs and also determined the legality of payment for government agents. The secretary of treasury was his nominal superior, but the solicitor had almost as much business with the attorney general as with the Treasury Department and ultimately was transferred to the Justice Department. The attorney general was in general charge of the administration of justice but was in constant conflict with United States district judges as to authority over the United States attorneys and their methods of presenting and prosecuting cases.[15]

The effective administration of slave trade laws was hampered by other problems as well. For example, Marshal Daniel H. Hamilton of Charleston (a physician), in caring for the *Echo's* Negroes at the order of President Buchanan, had incurred bills totaling $7,650 and requested reimbursement but was unable to get his money. In December he asked for funds to investigate the *Wanderer* Negroes kept in South Carolina. He received permission to incur "reasonable expenses," but because of the government's failure to pay him for his *Echo* expenses he was unwilling to spend more of his own money.[16]

Neither President Buchanan nor Attorney General Jeremiah Black appeared concerned over the *Wanderer,* but indifference was not true of Secretary of the Treasury Howell Cobb. One of Cobb's first moves was to get Henry Rootes Jackson, his half-brother and most active political supporter, an appointment as special United States attorney for the *Wanderer* cases. Jackson, a prominent Savannah lawyer belonging to the firm of Ward, Jackson, and Jones, had only recently relinquished the position of United States minister to Austria. He had been United States attorney for the Georgia district and was well known for his eloquent speeches and his poetry. Jackson was ambitious, imaginative, and a bit officious. From the beginning he and Ganahl had differences of opinion as to how to prepare and try the case, and, unfortunately, they did not receive explicit instructions outlining their responsibilities and defining the government's attitude. Neither was clearly in charge.

Jackson's lifelong contention was that the *Wanderer* enterprise was only a small segment of a big Yankee-directed conspiracy. His strategy was to broaden the case in order to discover and implicate Northern participants. Joseph Ganahl wanted to restrict the case to the few active offenders against whom he could marshal overwhelming evidence and get convictions.

A hearing for Corrie, Brown, Rajesta, and Arguivi was held beginning December 18, 1858, before United States Commissioner Charles S. Henry,[17] with Ganahl and Jackson representing the United States and the Savannah firm of Lloyd and Owens pleading for the defense.

The government attempted to promote a cleavage among the conspirators in an effort to secure the testimony of one against the other. Ganahl tried to get Judge Henry to rule that transportation along the Atlantic coast of a Negro already illegally introduced was not an offense. He was unsuccessful in this, but his point was understood by James Clubb and Luke Christie: Ganahl would not bring charges against them if they would testify against the principal offenders. Clubb at first refused to state his occupation on grounds that it might tend to incriminate him. A threat of jail for contempt changed his mind. Clubb and Christie, witnesses against Corrie, Brown, Rajesta, and Arguivi, also implicated Charles Lamar so far that he, too, was arrested, but since he was not charged with piracy he was allowed bail. Lamar told the authorities at Savannah that Corrie (who seems to have been in Charleston at this time) would surrender if allowed bail, but this Ganahl refused. A warrant was made out for Corrie's arrest. All five were bound over for the April session of the United States circuit court.[18]

Proceedings were started against the yacht and her tackle and furniture on January 26, 1859, before United States District Judge John C. Nicoll acting as a court of admiralty. Testimony and arguments were by written depositions, and no jury was involved. The case was simple and uncontested.[19] Charles Lamar wrote his father, "I am very much afraid the yacht will be confiscated . . . it is necessary in filing the answer to the libel to deny the accusations *under oath* . . . or give bond for all the cost and refuse to answer, upon the ground of implicating yourself. . . ."[20]

It was shown through depositions by Horatio Harris, James Clubb, and Luke Christie that African slaves had been illegally landed within the United States district of south Georgia. Reports later had it that Lamar offered Clubb and Harris $5,000 apiece not to testify, but the government outbid him. The only person whose ownership could be proven was William C. Corrie, whose name appeared on the Charleston registry as owner on June 8, 1858, and who now claimed only a one-eighth share; his partners remained silent. On February 25, 1859, Nicoll decreed that the *Wanderer,* having been owned, fitted out, and operated by a citizen of the United States for the purpose of procuring and introducing Negro slaves into the United States from Africa, and having committed these acts, was forfeited to the United States and condemned to be sold at auction in fifteen days.[21]

VI

Legal Maneuvers

DURING MANY periods in American history one great social and moral question has so thoroughly filled the attitudes and politics of the period that no field of endeavor can be discovered into which that one question did not enter. In 1858 the question was slavery. Everybody, every event, every move, was associated with this question. The senatorial election of 1858 in Illinois, legally free of slavery since 1787, was fought over the question. The campaign was waged as the Lincoln-Douglas debates. Lincoln lost this election, but Douglas in winning lost so much favor in the Southern wing of his Democratic party that Lincoln won the presidency in 1860. A Northerner or a Westerner could not hold Southern votes by moderation. Militancy was an absolute necessity in local or regional elections. It began to be necessary for Northerners to polarize for or against slavery in the same way that Southerners had already polarized. Throughout all the legal maneuvering and public utterances concerning the *Wanderer* lay the national argument over slavery and the problem of Southern unity in the face of abolitionist onslaughts.

In the weeks following the landing of the Africans, Charles Lamar was faced with numerous problems which he met with speed, vigor, and competence. At the same time he had to eliminate, silence, or discredit witnesses and do away with evidence. And, since trials appeared inevitable, he must get the public officials, possible jurors, and the general public into an appropriate frame of mind for his cause. His most immediate problem was the distribution of the cargo without getting caught or incurring excessive expense.

Lamar left about half the cargo behind on Jekyll Island for distribution, apparently by his friend Nelson Trowbridge. The fact that seventy years later some of the *Wanderer* people still lived on or near Jekyll Island leads one to believe that the Dubignons took at least part of the payment for use of their island in trade even if they were not outright share-holders in the enterprise. Newspaper rumors gave the rental fee for the island at $15,000.

Other newspapers North and South told of rumor or fact concerning movement of Africans from Jekyll Island. As early as January 8, 1859, *Harper's Weekly* had a fairly accurate feature article on the *Wanderer,* complete with a drawing. The following article in the *Marion Commonwealth* about the transfer of thirty-eight Africans to Montgomery by rail and downriver on the steamer *St. Nicholas* is probably a fair description of all the coffles that went by water:

I was carried through Brown's speculator house (so called) on Perry Street. In a house in the back lot where huddled together *thirty-eight native* (Congo) *Africans!* Don't shudder and say "The moral sentiments of Christendom condemn the traffic." But it is a fact; I have seen the Africans! And it is a fact—they were Africans!

I found them jabbering, in guttural sounds, something—I could not comprehend what. They were nearly all apparently in good health—fat, sleek and greasy. In the party were some five or six men, two or three women, four or five girls, and the rest boys, or what might be called "youngsters." They were each clad in common Kersey pants and roundabout over which they wore a heavy blanket. Women and all were thus dressed. None had shoes, for the reason that they could not walk in them; in fact, they could scarcely walk at all, having been confined and crowded so close on shipboard.

Most of them were very pert and lively, laughing and talking in their native tongue, and pointing at and jabbering about everything that particularly attracted their attention. Some of them had very singularly shaped craniums—they almost baffle description. One nearly square, one had a convex face, and another a sort of double concave convex head; but most of them had good heads, large flat noses, big mouths, front teeth knocked out, rather small ears, and quite small hands and feet. Some of them were good looking, but others shockingly ugly; some were what might be vulgarly called "puff" or hog-jawed. I noticed one, a man, who had very high cheek-bones and several scars on his face, and appeared very intelligent. He was "big chief" no doubt, in his country. I was much surprised at one thing; they repeated precisely every word said to them. I asked one, "Where did you come from?" and he propounded the same interrogatory to me, but of course without knowing the meaning and in like manner many other things.

Not being able to walk, they were carried in a wagon from the rail-road depot to Brown's, and thence by wagon to the St. Nicholas. I saw strong old farmers and sober-sided merchants gazing at the sable creatures, some of them having, no doubt, a holy horror at such a sight. The negroes were well skilled in pantomine, and some of them gave unmistakeable signs that they wanted "something to drink"—putting both hands to their mouths and throwing their heads back. The thirty-eight Africans brought here were the share, as I learned, in the venture of a citizen of New Or-leans, and that they cost him, delivered at Savannah, $50 each—only $1,900 for thirty-eight Africans, sound and able-bodied negroes. They were in charge of a Mr. Brodnax, who was carrying them to New Orleans. I said that the negroes were "all well." So they are, as well as could be expected, but, as might be conjectured, they were mostly suffering much from disorders incident to acclimation.

For some time the Africans could not be induced to go on board the boat, and seemed much frightened at the smoke, &c. Doubtless they had a perfect horror of travelling on the water again, after having so recently endured a long and crowded sea voyage. The manner in which they were finally induced to go on is worthy of notice. The mate tried every means to get them on board, but to no effect. Finally he concerted a plan with a big, black Alabama negro. He tried to get him to go on board, but he resolutely refused, when the mate laid him down on the gangway-plank, and hit him four or five substantial licks with his ponderous leather strap, when the said Alabama negro got up, yelling awfully, and went straight on board, beckoning to the Africans to follow. And they did follow, to the amusement, and amid the cheers of the crowd.[1]

One group turned up in south Georgia under Lamar's friend Richardson F. Aiken, who was an officer of the Savannah Jockey Club and a member of the Savannah regatta.

Deputy Marshal John F. McRae heard of a coffle of African slaves traveling through south Georgia headed west. He had already asked Marshal Stewart what to do in case he discovered any of the *Wanderer's* cargo. Stewart told McRae that he had not been able to get any instructions from Washington but that he proposed to confiscate any African blacks he encountered and supposed McRae might as well do likewise. Inasmuch as Negroes could not testify against white men in capital cases, their use to the prosecution was as evidence, that is, as people whose origin could prove that Afri-cans had been brought in.

McRae formed a posse consisting of ten men, including Alexan-der Dopson and his son Robert. He led them 60 miles south into Worth County until on March 1, 1859, they encountered Aiken leading a caravan of thirty-six African Negroes, three wagons, twelve mules, and some domestic slaves named Reuben, Cyrus, Charles, and John, who were helping to look after the Africans.

McRae seized the thirty-six Africans along with three of their legally enslaved caretakers (John, for some reason, was left behind), the three wagons, twelve mules, and other equipment, and took them to the Telfair County jail in Jacksonville, 60 miles from the point of seizure. After two days Aiken was released and allowed to take the three American-born Negroes and the equipment to the plantation of his friend Woodson Willcox two miles out of town.

McRae planned to turn the Negroes over to state authorities for disposition under an 1817 Georgia law intended to wreck the finances of slave smugglers by providing that the governor could sell such blacks to the general public or to the American Colonization Society for repatriation. McRae once more asked Stewart for instructions. Stewart telegraphed and wrote Washington again (apparently the attorney general) but, getting no reply, directed McRae to release his captives.

Richardson Aiken paid the county for the boarding of his charges, gathered them together, and started west. At the edge of town Alexander and Robert Dopson held up the party at gunpoint, grabbed the three domestic Negroes, and demanded $300 from Aiken, presumably after failing to get it from the county as payment for their part and expenses in making the seizure. Aiken refused. Colonel Paine, a prominent citizen, leaped in with $50.00 for the Dopsons to prevent bloodshed, and Aiken continued on his way. Two of his charges had sore feet and were dropped at the Willcox plantation for recuperation and treatment.

Edwin Gordon, the same assistant marshal who had seized the African boy on Jekyll Island, now posing as "Mr. Williams," went without search warrant to Willcox's house and saw the Negroes. Willcox discovered Gordon's identity; they shouted insults at each other across the highway, but the Africans were not taken. When Willcox was charged with "holding two Africans," a grand jury found "no bill." By the time Willcox was called as a witness he had fled to Texas and could not be found. Nor could the Africans be located.[2]

A few months later McRae, the Dopsons, and others were called to Savannah to testify before a grand jury considering indictment of Lamar and Aiken. Before they could get to court Lamar had them arrested for stealing Cyrus, Charles, and Reuben. Jackson and Ganahl thought they had Lamar cornered here because in order to prove ownership of the three American Negroes he might

be trapped into testifying in court concerning ownership of the
36-man African coffle. The deputy assigned to go to dinner with
the McRae group got drunk, failed to keep the United States attorneys informed about activities around the courthouse, and Marshal Stewart went their bond; they got out of jail without the
hearing the government lawyers wanted.[3] Although Charles Lamar
evaded self-incriminating testimony, the Dopsons and McRae gave
enough evidence to help bring about a grand jury indictment of
Lamar and Richardson Aiken for holding those thirty-six African
Negroes.

The group of about 170 Negroes brought past Savannah in the
Lamar and then reshipped to the Hamburg area in the *Augusta*
was conspicuous and should have been easily seized. It was a large
group, it was kept together in a well-settled area, and it included
a number of sick, some of whom died. Also, Lamar was busy deal-
ing with outsiders who wanted to syphon off some of the profits.
He wrote to his father: "I am afraid the parties or some of them
near Hamburg, will steal *all* they have. You never heard of so many
deaths in your life. One man by the name of Tillman, refuses to
give them up on any terms . . ."[4]

Tillman later demanded the delivery to him of two of the slaves
for the low price of $300. Lamar had a hard time keeping his
associates from becoming panic-stricken as the law began pressing
closer. It was only with effort that he prevented cut-rate prices for
the Africans from wiping out much of the profits. When a newspaper said that the price had fallen to $250, Lamar offered $450
for any brought in.[5]

Gumbo and Cuffee, the two "greenies" brought from Macon into
Savannah under heavy guard, remained in the county jail for
several months. As they could probably be proven Africans they
were a threat to the conspiracy. Lamar took action in a character-
istically bold and coldly contemptuous fashion. On March 8, 1859,
he waited until the federal court was in session and then went to
Magistrate John A. Staley petitioning for a writ of possession for
his two slaves. He brought along John F. Tucker, one of his associates, who swore that Gumbo and Cuffee were in Lamar's possession in December, 1858, which was true.

Staley sent for the county jailor, Charles Van Horn, who at first
refused to come. Then Constable Buckner forced him to come to
court. Van Horn protested that Cuffee and Gumbo were federal
prisoners. Lamar wanted his property. Van Horn asked that United

States Attorney Ganahl be sent for. Lamar still demanded his property. Van Horn offered to go get Ganahl but was denied permission to do so. Staley allowed Stewart and another man to go but they found the federal attorney unavailable because court was in session. After waiting about twenty minutes Staley went on with proceedings. Marshal Stewart said that the United States had no interest in Gumbo or Cuffee. They were turned over to Lamar as his legal possessions. Later, when Associate Supreme Court Justice James Wayne considered this sequestering of evidence, he vehemently pronounced the proceedings before Staley as illegal, but that did not secure Gumbo and Cuffee, who were seen no more in court.[6]

On April 15, 1859, true bills were found by the grand jury, United States circuit court, southern district of Georgia, against Charles Lamar, Richardson Aiken, John F. Tucker, and Randolph L. Mott. On April 22 John Dubignon, Henry Dubignon, and Nelson Trowbridge were similarly indicted. They were ordered to be tried.[7]

Lamar knew that they were to be tried before juries composed of local men, not of Northern newspapermen, definitely not of Northern politicians. He had good advice from lawyer R. I. Moses of Columbus. Lamar wrote to his father that Moses "advises the employment of prudence and no violence and the manufacture of Public Opinion by the employment of a man North to collate every act of injustice done to Southerners through their slave property in the last ten years and to crowd the Savannah papers with these extracts . . ."[8] The objective was to make the trial into a contest between Southern rights and Northern oppression. It was done well. The more the Northern newspapers attacked, the less likely were Southern juries to convict the conspirators.

Perhaps the main issue favoring Lamar's strategy was a Southern urge to regional unity. By 1859 Southern politicians generally agreed that internal splits had to be avoided at all costs. In order not to lose the strength that firebrands like Lamar lent to local unity they would avoid condemnation of their actions. This was the opinion of Congressman William Porcher Miles of South Carolina, of numerous correspondents of Senator Chesnut of South Carolina, and of many lesser men. Public opinion, or at least public utterances and actions, began to favor Lamar and his enterprise. The only signs of Southern disapproval were silence and the worried letters from Lamar's father. During the hearings before Commis-

sioner Henry, Charles Lamar was elected president of the Ten
Broek Races and was made a director of the Savannah, Albany
and Gulf Railroad.

William Price, the Northern-born tailor who reported the sale of
clothing to Brown and his sailors, was subject to such harrassment
that he published a declaration of his love of slavery in order to
save his business. In Edgefield a Northern woman was ordered out
of town and a church resolution condemning the introduction of
the *Wanderer's* slaves was withdrawn after pressure was brought
upon church members.

Lamar had powerful support in Savannah. There is no direct
evidence that United States Marshal Daniel Stewart was an active
member of the *Wanderer* conspiracy, but there can be no doubt
that he was useful to it. When Henry Rootes Jackson entered the
case he tried to replace Stewart, but this took three months to
accomplish and by then the damage was done. In one instance
Jackson discovered twenty-one Africans passing through Savannah
and directed Stewart to seize them. Stewart claimed he took orders
only from District Attorney Ganahl, telegraphed Washington as
was his custom when he did not want to do something, delayed, and
never acted. The twenty-one continued on through Savannah and
disappeared from the hold of the law.[9] It was Stewart who told
Deputy Marshal McRae to release the thirty-six Africans he captured. It was Stewart who persuaded McRae and his posse to avoid
the hearing which would have proved Lamar's ownership of the
Africans. It was Stewart who allowed Cuffee and Gumbo's release.

By order of Marshal Stewart the three *Wanderer* crewmen,
Brown, Rajesta, and Arguivi, were given every comfort in the jail
while awaiting action by the grand jury of the United States district
court of Georgia. The jailer carried their trunk in for them and
ran little errands such as buying claret, butter, sweet oils, and
cigars. They ran up bills occasionally totaling over a hundred
dollars a month which they paid through Mr. Molina, a tobacconist.
To reduce dampness in their cell, a new floor was laid at county
expense.[10]

Stewart was politically powerful and he wanted to keep his job
as United States marshal as well as his position as city marshal.
Jackson's candidate, James Spullock of Rome, Georgia, was drawing a nice salary as special investigator, and he took his time about
posting bond for the better-paying, prestigious but controversial
position as United States marshal. Stewart kept the job until March
14, 1859. After he left office he was an active supporter of William

B. Gaulden when the latter ran for Congress on a pro-slave-trade platform.

Two days before Spullock qualified, Stewart held the auction of the *Wanderer*, her tackle, furniture and lading, and goods and effects found on board of her at the time of her seizure. The sale took place on the northwest corner of the custom house where a big crowd gathered, including Charles Lamar and some of his rowdy friends. Someone, possibly Lamar, announced that the yacht was rightfully Lamar's. When the bidding started Lamar's only opponent was the jailer, Charles Van Horn. Van Horn bid $4,000. Lamar topped it with $4,001. Stewart knocked it down at once to Lamar, and Lamar at once knocked Van Horn down. There was some talk among the crowd of teaching Van Horn a lesson, but Lamar thought he had had enough.[11] Stewart followed instructions literally, turning over not only yacht and tackle, but also Corrie's trunk, charts, and personal papers. Half an hour after the sale, Lamar came to Van Horn at the jail and, according to Van Horn, "made a sort of apology—such an apology as he generally makes." In reply Van Horn "told him we would drop it for the present. Never had another word with him on the subject."[12]

A New England visitor to Savannah named Hazzard wrote home about the incident and an account appeared in a Rhode Island newspaper over his name. This story had Gumbo and Cuffee being sold with the yacht, Lamar claiming ownership of the *Wanderer*, and a group of Lamar's friends helping Lamar beat up jailer Van Horn. The Hazzard article quickly got back to Savannah. Lamar looked up Hazzard and gave the astonished Yankee a sharp slap with the back of his hand to lay the way open to a duel.[13]

Hazzard calmed Lamar down enough to find out what the trouble was and then explained that he had written a private letter home and that the recipient must have given it to a reporter who introduced the errors into it. Lamar felt his honor had been vindicated and that Hazzard should not be pushed further.

The *Savannah Daily Morning News* printed an account which got things nicely stirred up again: after Lamar slapped Hazzard and offered to fight a duel, he ordered Hazzard to leave town. The Northern press loved it; Lamar was a dictator who could run people out of town and did so.[14] A reliable source in New York [Gazaway Lamar?] wrote to the editor of the *New York Times* that Hazzard had not been ordered out of town. The writer went on to say how well his home town thought of Charles Lamar.[15] This letter seems to have quieted the New York newspapers, but Charles Lamar was not quiet. He wrote to both William Raymond of the *New York Times* and Horace Greeley of the *New York Herald,* demanding duels. When he could not get replies from either man, he wrote Congressman Lucius Q. C. Lamar to arrange a duel.[16] These efforts failed, but Charles Lamar gained considerable stature with many prospective jurors by making busybody Yankees back down or shut up. Every scornful article from the North predicting that Southern juries would be prejudiced for the defendants made that situation more likely to occur. No surer means for an acquittal could be arranged than for Northerner to insult the integrity of Southern juries.

A few days after the Hazzard incident, Lamar seized another chance to bedevil the Northern press and to ridicule an important United States official and key government witness against Lamar. He drove his sorrel mare Lady and his new $360 New York buggy to downtown Savannah. Beside him was a smart, alert little Negro boy. Ostentatiously he proceeded to introduce the boy as "Corrie." When Collector John Boston tried to look the other way Lamar loudly asked him if he wanted to meet a genuine African from the *Wanderer.* Boston said and did nothing. Lamar took "Corrie" to church, boasting himself the best missionary of the age.[17] Bystanders got another laugh at the impotence of a law officer who was merely trying to avoid trouble. Prestige of federal officials in Savannah was under serious and sustained attack. There is no telling whether "Corrie" was actually a recent importation. Charles Lamar liked to make a good show, but it is doubtful that he would take a chance of being arrested in the company of one of the *Wanderer's* cargo.

The money from the sale of the yacht was paid into the court which awarded $849.36 to Stewart and $57.50 to Ganahl for expenses, $63.25 for fees, and the remainder to Woodford Mabry as informer. Solicitor General Hillyer objected to Mabry's award. He believed that government officials ashore, unlike naval crews at sea, were not entitled to rewards for service performed in the line of duty. Nevertheless, Mabry kept the money.[18]

In the meantime, Lamar's *E. A. Rawlins* was in the news. About December 13, 1858, Lamar sent the *Rawlins* with a cargo of rice and possibly with some of the *Wanderer's* fleeting crew from Savannah to Havana. She then cleared Havana for Mantua to pick up a load of fruit. In March, 1859, she was discovered in lonely St. Joseph Bay on the west Florida coast. Captain Horace H. Hayden called himself Captain Hill and his vessel the *Rosalie,* but the identity of each was soon discovered. An unlikely rumor said that the vessel had landed nine hundred slaves. Other stories told of desertion by part of the crew, of illegal sale and delivery of the vessel, and of murder of a Spanish captain whose body was thrown overboard. The truth seems to be that the *E. A. Rawlins* had been sold to someone for use in the slave trade. In order to conceal true ownership (a usual tactic of slave ship owners), the transfer of title was to be made at sea. Apparently the crew did not wish to make a slave voyage. Attempts to drug the prospective captain having failed, he was attacked and accidentally killed. Second Mate Sloan was tried, convicted of manslaughter, and sentenced to five years imprisonment and a $1,000 fine. The first mate was acquitted. Captain Hayden leaped over the side and escaped. The *E. A. Rawlins* was seized, condemned for being fitted as a slaver, and sold for $9,000. Charles Lamar was not present; nobody was knocked down at the auction.[19]

Three times United States authorities in Savannah tried to get William C. Corrie arrested in Charleston. Each time the United States judge for South Carolina, Andrew G. Magrath, thwarted them. First, Joseph Ganahl sent a request that a bench warrant be issued on behalf of the United States district court meeting in Savannah. Nothing was done.[20] Next, Ganahl appeared in person. Judge Magrath issued a warrant, but for his own court. When William Corrie was finally persuaded to come to court, he was allowed to make bond even though he was charged with piracy, a capital offense.[21] At last, May 19, 1859, he was brought before a federal grand jury in Charleston. The hearing was presided over by Associate Justice James M. Wayne of the United States Supreme Court and by Magrath, acting as a United States circuit court, that type of court being specifically designated for piracy cases tried under the act of May 15, 1820. The grand jury found no bill against Corrie. Wayne dismissed the jury, and Ganahl prepared to claim Corrie for his own court.[22]

Charlestonians had no intention of permitting Corrie, a fellow South Carolinian, to be tried in an atmosphere less sympathetic than theirs. The foreman of the grand jury, Edward Sebring, said that the jury wanted to reconsider the bill. Wayne pointed out that the grand jury had already been dismissed. Magrath agreed, adding that, unlike a presentment, an indictment could not now be received. Sebring got the hint. The jury asked for information about presentments. This brought up the constitution, and nobody loved to talk about the constitution more than Charleston lawyers. The present-

ment (a seldom-used method by which a grand jury on its own
initiative originates a criminal charge) was received, Corrie's bond
increased to $10,000, and Ganahl had to return to Savannah with-
out his prisoner.[23]

Judge Magrath had recently come in contact with slave-trade
law violations in the *Echo* and the *Brothers* cases. The *Echo* had
been caught August 21, 1858, by the United States brig-of-war
Dolphin just off the coast of Cuba as she was preparing to land her
African slaves. Her captain, Edward N. Townsend, was taken
first to Key West, then to Boston, aboard the *Dolphin*. The *Echo*
with her crew and slaves was sent to Charleston under a prize crew.
The *Echo's* entire crew was charged with piracy. The Negroes were
kept at Fort Sumter, turned over to the American Colonization
Society for repatriation, and returned to Africa aboard the U.S.S.
Niagara.

Charles Lamar heard of the repatriation plans when his *Wanderer*
was approaching the Congo River. He wrote the *Savannah Daily
Morning News:*

Mr. Editor: I see in your issue of this morning that "the American
Colonization Society has offered to take the captured Africans, on landing
in Liberia, and for $50,000 keep them for one year and learn them
industrial pursuits." Now, I desire to make this proposition to the Government; I will take them and give $50,000 for the privilege, and will
guarantee to teach them "industrial pursuits" without any charge, and
keep them for a term of years. Which proposition will the Government
accept? They are much in want of money, but equally in need of popularity *North,* and I am inclined to think they will favor the Society that
Judge Lumpkin, of our Supreme Court, has denounced as a swindle. We
shall soon see.[24]

C. A. L. Lamar

The *Echo's* crew was brought before a grand jury of the circuit
court at Charleston with Leonidas W. Spratt as their attorney. A
specialist in this type of case, Spratt contended that laws declaring
overseas slave-trade piracy were unconstitutional. Further, he insisted that they were an infringement upon a state's right to determine its own criminal law, and that the slave-trade laws were
imposed on a minority by a tyrannous majority.

Judge Wayne, as requested by United States Attorney James
Conner, instructed the jury that constitutionality of laws was a matter to be determined not by them but by judicial authorities. The
grand jury brought out an indictment, but when the members of

the crew were tried on April 16, 1859 (the month before the Corrie hearings), they were found not guilty.[25]

Captain Townsend was taken before Judge Sprague in Boston. Sprague decided that the Florida district had jurisdiction and ordered Townsend returned to Key West. There the prosecution could not prove to Judge William Marvin that the *Echo* was an American vessel. Her registry did not prove a thing; anybody might use a registry as a blind for the real owner. The prosecution produced a bill of sale. Judge Marvin, reputed to be one of the greatest admiralty judges in our history, said there was no one to swear that it had been executed and refused to allow the case to be postponed long enough to produce seller or witness. He charged the jury that American ownership of the *Echo* had not been proved. Townsend was freed.[26]

This line of reasoning was followed in the *Wanderer* cases.

The case of the ketch *Brothers* was somewhat different. The *Brothers* had not yet embarked slaves when she was seized off Africa by the United States sloop-of-war *Marion* in September, 1858, while the *Wanderer* was nearby, but she did have slaving equipment aboard. In the case of the crew, Magrath charged the grand jury that such equipment was not clearly and solely designed for slave-catching and in the absence of other evidence did not prove her a slaver. The grand jury ignored the bill against the crew. Later, in admiralty proceedings against the vessel, Magrath similarly ruled that even though there was suspicion that she was going into the slave trade there was reasonable doubt as to her mission. He returned her to her owners.[27]

In addition to the legal precedents set and the judicial frames of mind illustrated, the *Echo* and *Brothers* trials had another important effect on the *Wanderer* trials. Law officers, as stated earlier, particularly the marshal, found it difficult to get their fees or even their expense money for their investigative work and for caring for the Negroes seized as evidence. As a result, Marshal Hamilton declined to go to the Hamburg-Edgefield area when there were numerous reports of *Wanderer* Africans there. It is possible he did not want to find evidence, but his actions are understandable in the light of his recent experience, and Hamilton appears an honorable and zealous marshal throughout the cases. He finally got money in 1860, but his accounts were still in doubt in 1868 over payments in the *Echo* case. Clearly, if the attorney general wanted a federal conviction he had to gather evidence and the collection was going to cost money which should come from federal sources. Attorney

General Jeremiah S. Black's actions in the *Echo* as well as the *Wanderer* cases make one doubt that he wanted a conviction. Black gave weak and uninterested support to the *Wanderer* prosecutions, as will be shown in the next two chapters. Faulty governmental organization and poorly written statutes contributed to these failures, but vigorous action by Black might have overcome these obstacles.

VII

Trials

THE HISTORY of the *Wanderer* trials is incomplete. Verbatim records of evidence were not kept. Newspaper accounts are subject to deliberate or unintentional errors and omissions. The Civil War came during a time when much of the legal review and recording would normally have taken place; after the war was over, slave-trade precedents were of academic, not practical, interest. Unquestionably, material dangerous to participants in the *Wanderer* venture was removed in order to prevent postwar prosecution and harassment. The account that follows, although incomplete and frequently supported only by newspaper stories, is probably as complete as is possible at the present time.

The *Wanderer* was libeled before Judge John C. Nicoll, acting as a United States admiralty court, for having violated portions of the act of April 20, 1818, which provided for the forfeiture of United States registered vessels involved in illegal slave trade. In admiralty cases no jury was required, testimony was written, and there was no question of jurisdiction. It merely had to be proved that the vessel was owned by a citizen of the United States and that she had introduced African slaves to the United States, or had been fitted out as a slaver. Corrie's proctor admitted Corrie owned a one-eighth share of the *Wanderer*. James Clubb's and Horatio Harris' testimony that the *Wanderer* had landed African Negroes was unchallenged and conclusive to the court. The *Wanderer* was declared forfeited on February 25, 1859.[1]

The piracy trials in Savannah were before the United States Sixth Circuit Court, presided over by Supreme Court Associate

Justice James M. Wayne and the local District Judge John C. Nicoll. The prosecutors were Henry Rootes Jackson, special assistant to the attorney general for the cases, and Joseph Ganahl, succeeded in 1860 by Hamilton Couper, United States attorney for the district of southern Georgia.

James M. Wayne had been appointed to the Supreme Court by President Andrew Jackson in 1835 as a reward for Wayne's congressional support during the South Carolina nullification crisis. Born in Savannah in 1790, Wayne had started his Supreme Court career under John Marshall. He was considered the Supreme Court's leading authority on admiralty law. Wayne had insisted that the court consider constitutional aspects of the Missouri Compromise in the Dred Scott case, and he voted with the majority in declaring that Congress could not prohibit slavery in the territories. Nevertheless, Wayne was a strong unionist in the secessionist controversy and remained an active member of the United States Supreme Court throughout the Civil War, although his son became a major general in the Georgia militia.

John C. Nicoll was born in Baldwin County, Georgia, in 1794 and lived in Savannah. He had been city recorder, judge of the city court, mayor, and judge of the Chatham Superior Court. He was appointed United States district judge in 1839. He, too, was a unionist, but he resigned from the bench in 1861 and later became the Confederate States attorney for the same district in which he had earlier been judge. Although Nicoll was Lamar's father-in-law he did not disqualify himself in the *Wanderer* cases. He took a much less prominent and aggressive part than did Judge Magrath of Charleston; Nicoll seems to have acted with great correctness and impartiality throughout all the trials of Lamar and the other defendants.

The trial of Nicholas Brown, Juan Bt. Rajesta, and Miguel Arguivi for piracy began November 12, 1859, two weeks after John Brown in Virginia had been convicted and sentenced to hang for his raid on Harper's Ferry. This decision met approval in the South and widespread disapproval in the North, particularly in literary and philosophical circles. When the *Wanderer* defendants won their cases, even Southerners who disapproved of their crimes cheered the verdicts as acts of defiance against Northern interference. Four panels were exhausted before a jury could be formed.

Jackson and Ganahl had three principal points to prove in order to convict the three men of piracy under the act of May 15, 1820:[2] *(a)* that the *Wanderer* was owned or chartered by an American citizen, *(b)* that the vessel had engaged in the overseas slave trade, *(c)* that Brown, Arguivi, and Rajesta were members of the *Wanderer's* crew while she was engaged in the slave trade.

Ownership of the vessel should have been easy to prove, in light of the condemnation proceedings the previous spring. However, the judges ruled that the findings of the previous trial were not admissible. It is normal procedure in capital cases that evidence from deposition is not used. While Corrie through his lawyer had admitted ownership in the prior case, the prosecution was now required to establish ownership independently of anything that had gone before. The government could produce only hearsay: Harris' report of his conversation with Corrie in the boat on the way to see Clubb; the testimony of the clerk for Hugh Vincent, the chandler, that Corrie had told him he paid $30,000 for the vessel; Napoleon Coste's testimony that Corrie had stated to him (Coste, captain of the revenue cutter at Charleston, knew Corrie well) that he was a part owner of the *Wanderer;* and J. Pinckney Walker's statement that Corrie reported himself to him as master and owner of the *Wanderer*. Corrie himself could not be brought into the Savannah court, and documentary evidence signed by him was not proved authentic.

Testimony of Horatio Harris, James Clubb, and Luke Christie proved that the *Wanderer* had landed a large number of Negroes. Testimony of Dr. Hazelhurst, Dr. Duke (physician for the Savannah River group of slaves), and Deputy Marshal Gordon was supposed to show that the Negroes were Africans.

Testimony of George Cheever and Mr. Blount who had examined her logs, charts, and books, indicated that the *Wanderer* had been off Africa, but the court ruled, as is still customary, that the logs could not be used against those who had kept them unless the writer identified them in court. Naturally Brown would not incriminate himself and Brooks could not be found.

Harris, Clubb, and Christie were not positive in their identification of the three accused and the government introduced a barber to testify that Brown's beard appeared to have been dyed black from its original red. Jackson implied that someone had been tampering with the witnesses, who, he claimed, had earlier been quite positive in their identifications. Owens challenged Jackson to prove that there had been pressure on the witnesses; no evidence of the sort was brought up. Yet, a year later Marshal Spullock's claim for "hazardous and extra" services included the statement, "during the whole time the greatest excitement prevailed and dur-

ing the two nights the Court House was surrounded by an excited
crowd and threats were made of mobbing the officers and had a
verdict of Guilty been rendered a rescue would have been attempted
at the risk of the life of every official who did his duty."[3]

It had to be proven that Brown, Rajesta, and Arguivi were members of the crew when the *Wanderer* carried slaves. When the
shipping master came from Charleston, his shipping list did not
show the names of the accused (they almost surely sailed under
aliases) and was not introduced in evidence. Napoleon Coste was
able to testify that he had seen Brown and Arguivi coming and
going to the *Wanderer* in July, 1858, in a manner indicating that
they belonged to the ship, but he did not know that these men
made the cruise to Africa and back in her. J. Pinckney Walker told
about the protection he had issued to Corrie and the one he had
given Corrie for Dennis, but Jackson was unable to connect Dennis
and Brown as the same man. His attempt to use Lucien Peyton
as a handwriting expert failed.

The case was therefore weak in establishing Brown, Arguivi,
and Rajesta as members of the *Wanderer's* crew. The fact that the
vessel brought in African slaves seemed fairly well proved. For
some reason the questioning of Dr. Duke was insulting, sarcastic,
and unbecoming gentlemen like Jackson and Ganahl. Duke apparently co-operated, but he would not say things he did not want to
say; more sympathetic questioning might have provided more
effective answers. The proof of American ownership could be
inferred by a jury hostile to the accused, rejected by an unbiased
jury, and laughed at by a jury that wanted to release the prisoners.
Owens' final argument was short, logical, forcible, and was addressed as much to the crowd as to the jury. Jackson followed with
a four-and-a-half-hour discourse in which he cited much law and
many authorities, legal and historical. He exhorted the members
of the jury to uphold the law, regardless of personal considerations.
Justice Wayne recessed the court before making his charge to
the jury.

The next day, November 22, 1859, Wayne delivered the charge.
He recited a history of federal action in connection with the slave
trade, laying particular stress on the fact that Southern statesmen
had led the movement to suppress it. He said that the accused were
"pretty plainly and conclusively shown to be connected with the
Wanderer."[4] The jury considered this case twenty hours and rendered a "not guilty" verdict at noon, November 23, 1859.[5]

The same jury considered charges against Nicholas Brown for

a lesser offense, "importing African Negroes" under the same evidence, in violation of sections 6 and 7 of the act of April 20, 1818.[6] These sections merely required proof of the fact that the accused participated in the overseas slave trade or else bought, sold, or held a slave so introduced. Since the charges would be so much easier to prove and since the penalty was much lighter, a conviction seemed more likely than in the piracy cases. After almost a full day of consideration the jury asked for a doctor to examine the foreman, Carl Epping. The judges sent for Dr. Sullivan, Epping's physician, who found his patient too sick to continue. A mistrial resulted. Rumor had it that the jurors were eight to four for conviction when Epping was incapacitated.[7] Nicholas Brown was released on $10,000 bail for trial in the April, 1860, session of the court.

A grand jury considered indictments against Arguivi and Rajesta for "importing African Negroes." No bill was found. Apparently the jury did not feel that the sailors had been clearly identified by the witnesses.

Jackson and Ganahl both submitted their resignations soon after these trials. There had been friction between them from the beginning of their association, and Jackson had written the United States attorney general for support of his contention that Ganahl was subject to his orders.[8] During the course of the trials Jackson had interjected questions to the witnesses so frequently that Judge Wayne had to direct that either one or the other do all the questioning of an individual witness. When it came to the final argument, Jackson had taken that critical time for himself. Ganahl must have felt that he was being used as a law clerk.[9] The extent of Jackson's authority (if any) over the United States attorney in either Georgia or South Carolina was never clearly defined by Attorney General Black or the President.

The new district attorney was Hamilton Couper, the thirty-year-old son of James Hamilton Couper of Hopeton Plantation near Brunswick. Hamilton Couper was an aesthetic young man with an interest in literature and poetry which might have made him more sympathetic toward Jackson than Ganahl had been.

When the April, 1860, session of the circuit court was held the docket was full of *Wanderer* cases. The following cases were scheduled, as violations of the act of April 20, 1818:

U. S. v. *C. A. L. Lamar* — Holding an African named Corrie

U. S. v. *C. A. L. Lamar* — Holding two Africans named Cuffee and Gumbo

U. S. v. C. A. L. Lamar and *Richardson F. Aiken* — Holding thirty
   six African negroes in Telfair County, including Poor Billy, John,
   Andrew, Shanghai Billy, Ishmael, Motu, Dick, Philango, Zig,
   and Jimmy
U. S. v. John F. Tucker — Holding African negroes
U. S. v. Randolph L. Mott — Holding an African negro boy
U. S. v. William R. Fleming — Holding African negroes
U. S. v. Henry Dubignon —-Holding African negroes
U. S. v. Nelson Trowbridge and *John Dubignon* — Holding and
   abetting in the holding of African negroes.

Before the jury was empaneled, Couper requested permission to
ask each juror if he had "any conscientious scruples against punishment by imprisonment" in the cases to be tried. Owens contended
that such questions could be asked only in capital cases. The judges
upheld Owens. Jackson, who had withdrawn his resignation, then
asked that the clerk give special instruction to the jurors to make
known to the court any prejudices they might have against imprisonment for engaging in the slave trade. This, too, was refused.[10]

The indictments were based on violations of section 6 of the act
of April 20, 1818.

A mistrial was declared in Trowbridge's case on May 15, after
the jury deliberated twenty-eight hours without a decision. John
Dubignon was found not guilty on May 17.

Charles Lamar's trial for violation of slave-trade laws was scheduled for May 25, 1860, but was postponed until May 28 to allow
the piracy case of J. Egbert Farnum to be completed. When finally
Lamar's trial began, Harris and Clubb testified once more about the
Wanderer's entry and delivery of slaves. Lamar's name was not
mentioned. Captain Christie told about taking Lamar, Trowbridge,
Tucker, and Brown to Jekyll Island and loading the Negroes, drop-
ping Lamar off above Savannah, and then disembarking the Negroes
at Tucker's direction. Captain Dickerson testified that Lamar had
tried to hire him before he got Christie, but that he had never heard
Lamar discuss the trip again. Captain Stevenson said Lamar had
hired the steamer *Lamar* from him. No witness was able to connect
Lamar more closely with the *Wanderer*.

The *Wanderer's* register, charts, log, and nautical calculations
were introduced to prove that the *Wanderer* had actually been to
Africa in the fall of 1858, and this time the defense agreed to their
being introduced without identification by their author.

It may have been common knowledge that Lamar was principal
owner of the *Wanderer* and ringleader of the conspiracy, but, as

Wayne warned Jackson and Couper, the testimony had not directly connected Lamar and the yacht. There was an alarming gap in the case that had to be remedied if a conviction were to be made. Unfortunately, the prosecution had nothing more to offer. At four-thirty on the afternoon of May 28, 1860, Hamilton Couper moved for a *nolle prosequi* (permission not to prosecute) in the cases of C. A. L. Lamar and then in the cases against R. F. Aiken, R. L. Mott, Henry Dubignon, and John F. Tucker, for holding African Negroes.[11]

Nicholas Brown and Nelson Trowbridge were released on bail while awaiting trial on charges respectively of importing African Negroes and holding African Negroes. Charges against Farnum and Corrie *(in absentia)* for piracy were continued until the November, 1860, term, and Farnum, too, posted bail. On November 12, 1860, Couper moved for a *nolle prosequi* on all four of these cases.[12]

Reaction of Savannah residents was reflected in the following editorial comment:

This abrupt termination of these trials was the subject of much remark on the street; but in view of the disturbance they have created in our community—often arraying friend against friend and the utter hopelessness of a conviction in the end, we believe all were gratified with the result. If Africans are to be imported, we hope in Heaven that no more will be landed on the shores of Georgia.[13]

Meanwhile, William C. Corrie remained out of the jurisdiction of the Savannah court. In Charleston Judge Andrew G. Magrath interpreted the act of May 15, 1820, as giving his court exclusive jurisdiction in Corrie's case since Corrie had first been arrested in South Carolina. Corrie was released on $5,000 bail, later increased to $10,000.

Magrath belonged to the extreme state's right group so prominent in Charleston. Born in Charleston in 1813, he had studied law under the Charleston unionist James L. Petigru and at Harvard Law School. He had been a state legislator for two terms and had been appointed a federal district judge in 1856. The United States attorney general wished to get Corrie's trial out of the South Carolina district. Since the other judge, Justice Wayne, was a member of both the Georgia and South Carolina courts, the desire to take the case to Savannah apparently reflected distrust of Magrath, fear of public opinion in South Carolina, or both. Magrath suggested before the *Echo* trials that the attorney general of the state of South Carolina be associated with the United States attorney for the case to show the jurors that "the law of the United States in this matter is the law of the states."[14]

On March 17, 1860, Attorney General Jeremiah S. Black directed that United States Attorney James Conner enter a *nolle prosequi* in the case against Corrie. Conner did so in an atmosphere electric with excitement over the split in the Democratic National Convention in another part of the city. Magrath, sitting alone in the case, asked Conner if instructions from the attorney general were his only reason for entering a *nolle prosequi*. Conner replied that it was. Magrath then issued rulings on two questions: the request for *nolle prosequi* and the definition of slave trade as piracy under the act of May 15, 1820.

Magrath denied the right of the attorney general to direct a district attorney to request a *nolle prosequi*. Magrath further ruled that a judge was not obliged to grant such a request, even if the president of the United States directed it. He surmised, he said, that the real reason for a *nolle prosequi* was to get Corrie out of his court so that he could be arrested for the United States court of the Georgia district for the lesser offense of holding African slaves. Once Corrie was re-arrested, Magrath said, it was the government's intention to re-enter piracy charges and try Corrie in Georgia for offenses it said it could not prove in Magrath's court. He denied the request for a *nolle prosequi*.[15]

The other question Magrath considered was the definition of piracy under the act of May 15, 1820. He said that piracy was the forcible and unlawful seizure of property, including the bodies of individuals, ashore by seamen. He did not consider the transfer of slaves from one master to another as piracy, any more than he would so consider transfer of other property legally purchased. The word "piracy" by common and ancient usage had a meaning to Magrath which a mere act of Congress could not change. Hence, the prosecution would have to prove that the slaves had been forcibly deprived of their liberty in order to prove piracy.

Henry Jackson then addressed the court and, stating that he had been instructed to act as associate counsel, asked that Corrie be released. The government, he said, could not prove piracy according to Magrath's definition and it would be futile to prosecute. Jackson had in his possession the original bill of sale for the *Wanderer* slaves. Magrath asked Conner for his comments. Conner said that he had not been told of Jackson's being associated with him in the case. He thought he should await instructions from the attorney general. Magrath agreed and recessed the court.[16]

On June 5, 1860, Conner made the following statement in the United States Circuit Court presided over by Wayne and Magrath:

At the commencement of this term, I received instructions from the Attorney-General of the United States to enter a Nol. Pros. in the case [*U. S.* v. *Corrie*] with a view to the removal of the accused to Savannah for trial. The action was made, and upon it His Honor, the District Judge ruled, refusing the entry of the Nolle Prosequi, and affirming exclusive jurisdiction over the case to be in this District. This is the present position of the cause. A full report of the proceeding had here, and a statement of every fact necessary to a perfect comprehension of the case has been submitted to the Attorney-General, and abundant time allowed for consideration. I am, however, without reply or instructions. This is the fourth term of the cause. We are now at the close of it, and if the term expire without some action taken, the accused will, I apprehend, be discharged by operation of law.

Such an irregular and improper termination of the cause would be a matter much to be regretted, but having done all that I could do, I do not feel myself in the slightest degree responsible for the result. The responsibility for it does not rest here but elsewhere. I have only now to move the discharge of the Grand Jury.

Justice Wayne then said, "Gentlemen of the Grand Jury, you are discharged according to the request of the District Attorney."[17]

Wayne's inaction in this case is curious. His charges to juries in both Savannah and Charleston were forthright to the point that he appeared prejudiced against the accused. He was an old man and a unionist, so his personal popularity should not have been a consideration. He had willingly contended with critical issues in the Dred Scott case of 1857. Why did he not get the Supreme Court to overrule Magrath and move the case to Savannah? Did the fiery, aggressive spirit of the vigorous young Magrath influence the elderly Wayne into permitting delay after delay until Corrie was finally freed? Or did Wayne wish to avoid a storm of criticism such as the one which came his way after the Dred Scott decision? Whatever the explanation, no move was then made to arrest Corrie in behalf of the Savannah court.

As for Magrath, he seems to have been baldly prejudiced and unfit to sit as United States circuit or district judge on slave-trade cases. In the *Echo* and *Brothers* cases he had already shown his intention of nullifying in court the various acts of Congress intended to stifle the slave trade. He continued to go beyond the bounds of propriety in Corrie's case. His actions were popular in Charleston; desire for adulation and political advantage may have been his principal motives; maybe he believed in the legalisms he used;

maybe he was carried away on the emotional binge Charleston indulged from 1858 to 1861. At any rate, his rulings and actions were of great importance to the *Wanderer* conspiracy. Before the trial Jackson wrote Cobb that he and Wayne both thought Magrath was completely prejudiced and that a trial of Corrie in Charleston would be a mockery. He further charged Attorney Black with failure to stand behind Jackson as over-all head of the prosecution of the *Wanderer* cases.[18]

On November 7, 1860, when Lincoln's election was certain, Magrath resigned from the bench and removed his robes in the courtroom. Conner followed him. Magrath became governor of South Carolina in 1864 and served to the end of the Confederacy.

Farnum has also been called the captain, though he does not seem to have the seagoing background for that position. It may be that Farnum was expected to assume military command if trouble developed, or his presence may have been part of a ruse to make people believe that the *Wanderer* was part of some new filibustering expedition. It appears probable that William Corrie acted as captain in social and official matters and that Nicholas Brown was the true mariner of the vessel. Such confusion over command was deliberate, planned, and usual among slavers, so that in case of capture evidence would be contradictory. When the slaver *Echo* was taken off Cuba and the boarding officer asked, "Who is captain?" the answer given with coolness and dignity was, "All are captains."[2]

Farnum left the *Wanderer* as soon as she got to Jekyll Island. Not a single witness reported seeing him while the *Wanderer* was being brought to her anchorage or afterward on the beach. Aboard the *Columbia* leaving Charleston for New York on December 15, 1858, he gave an interview to an Albany reporter who was on the steamer.[3] Another journalist who saw him soon afterward on the street in Washington reported: "Behind [General Henningsen] struts 'the Wanderer,' Capt. J. E. Farnum, with an unholy odor, not of rosemary but of ebony, clinging to his clothes and beard."[4]

According to Jackson, Attorney General Jeremiah S. Black was in April, 1859, approached by a New York lawyer who said that Farnum proposed to supply Black "with the log book of the *Wanderer,* and with evidence enough to convict the men you are now prosecuting, for $7,000, to be paid after conviction; himself, of course, to enjoy immunity." This was an invitation for the attorney general of the United States to commit the impropriety of paying a witness a large sum of money for his testimony. Black asked for Jackson's opinion. Jackson said he did not think it honorable for the government to enter such an arrangement; he proposed arresting Farnum immediately. Black replied that he promised not to disclose the offer, and he refused to allow Jackson to act.

Jackson returned to Savannah and got grand jury indictments against all known conspirators except Farnum, whom he expected to be arrested and tried in New York. Theodore Sedgwick, United States attorney for the southern district of New York, came to Savannah and Jackson furnished him documents and lists of witnesses Jackson thought adequate for Farnum's conviction. When Sedgwick, who was very ill (he died during May, 1859), failed to get Farnum arrested, Jackson recovered his documents. In November Brown, Rajesta, and Arguivi were found not guilty of piracy.

Jackson resigned. Not only was he disappointed at the jury's verdict, but he also felt he was not being fully supported by Attorney General Black. Jackson said that his vigorous prosecution of the cases in Savannah with no corresponding activity in New York made it appear that Savannah was the center of the slave-trade conspiracy rather than New York. Further, he said, "Farnum, the leader in the *Wanderer* expedition, was notoriously in New York City, and not arrested."

Jackson says that President Buchanan sent for him and told him that Jackson was wrong in believing the government was uninterested in arresting Farnum. It was "a singular fact that Farnum can not be arrested." Jackson volunteered to get a special agent and seize the rascal himself. The President agreed. Jackson chose Lucien Peyton, a Patent Office employee who used to be a pension fraud investigator and handwriting expert.

Jackson and Peyton went to New York and got United States District Judge Betts to issue a bench warrant for Farnum's arrest. Marshal Isaiah Rynders, the same man who had allowed Corrie to sail the *Wanderer* out of New York in June, 1858, arrested Farnum but kept him in his own home. Next day, accompanied by Peyton, the marshal's nephew Theodore, and two other guards, Jackson took Farnum to Washington where Theodore Rynders and his friends got drunk or pretended to and, but for Peyton's watchfulness, would have allowed Farnum's escape. Peyton continued to Savannah with Farnum. At Augusta he changed his plans at the last minute and went by rail instead of by steamboat, thus frustrating a plan (later reported by Jackson) to release Farnum by force. Judge Nicoll refused Farnum bail and placed him in jail.

When Jackson returned to Savannah he found that Farnum had denounced him from the county jail, had defied him to prove his story, and had threatened to kill Jackson if he got out. Jackson went down to the jail and interviewed Farnum. Farnum swore he had witnesses who could disprove Jackson's claim that Farnum had offered to turn state's evidence against his associates for money. Jackson reported that he offered to pay the expenses and to give his personal assistance to bring Farnum's witnesses forward in Washington but that Farnum failed to produce them. But the burden of proof lay with Jackson, not Farnum.

Jackson told the attorney general that his bluff had been called and that he must now produce the New York lawyer who was intermediary between Farnum and Attorney General Black. Black said that unfortunately he did not know the man's name. The only help he could give was to sketch the man's nose, a most remarkable feature. Jackson set Lucien Peyton looking for an attorney with an unusual nose, and surprisingly Peyton found him, Mr. Marshall Bacon.

Jackson secured permission for Peyton to make an almost unlimited investigation of the suspected conspiracy. Peyton toured New England, New York, and the South looking for evidence. The President and the attorney general continued to offer help to Jackson in these investigations and to ask for specific recommendations. Jackson was able to reply only with general accusations. Peyton's reports consisted mostly of supporting claims for travel vouchers.[5]

Farnum was finally brought to trial in Savannah on May 21, 1860. It was difficult to select a jury, particularly as Justice Wayne allowed the prospective jurymen to be asked whether they had conscientious scruples against the infliction of capital punishment in the case. So many persons had scruples that it took three panels to make up a jury. Harris, Clubb, Christie, and others were on the witness stand on the morning and early afternoon of May 22 giving their usual testimony.

At last came Marshall Bacon's turn. The long-nosed lawyer readily admitted that he had transmitted an offer to Attorney General Jeremiah S. Black "to furnish, for a consideration (the sum of $5,000 or $7,000) testimony to convict the parties implicated in the *Wanderer* affair." However, Bacon denied that he was working with or for Farnum and he likewise declined to name the person who was involved. There is nothing to show that the court tried to force him to implicate anyone.

The next witness was Edwin Ward Moore, late commander in chief of the navy of the Republic of Texas, who testified that Farnum had told him about participation in a slaving voyage aboard the *Wanderer*. Moore's damaging testimony threatened the conspiracy. Had Farnum's trial come a year earlier the testimony might have led to conviction, but this was the election year 1860 and Southern feelings were running high.

Moore finished about 8:00 P.M. and the court recessed until the next day. As Moore walked toward the vestibule he was accosted by Charles Lamar, who, with his friends looking on expectantly, loudly proclaimed Moore a liar. Moore pulled out his notebook, calmly and insultingly asked Lamar his name, and arranged a duel.

United States Attorney Hamilton Couper acted as Moore's second and Lawyer John Owens acted for Lamar. Next morning on the popular dueling ground at Screven's Ferry across the Savannah River in South Carolina, Moore announced to his party that since Charles Lamar's cousin Mirabeau B. Lamar, whose Texas presidential term was sandwiched between Sam Houston's two terms, had been Moore's friend and benefactor, Moore would not kill Lamar, merely shoot him through the right shoulder. Moore's bullet whizzed within an inch of Lamar's right ear and shoulder. Lamar missed widely. His second apologized on his behalf. Moore examined his pistol. The seconds had failed to replace the rammer after loading and the weapon was thrown out of balance. Lamar later wrote that he intentionally fired wild.[6]

After two barbers and Commissioner Henry also gave testimony of an unknown nature for the defense, S. Yates Levy, Farnum's attorney, spoke for three hours and Henry Jackson followed. Levy's principal emphasis lay on the unconstitutionality of the act of May 15, 1820. He denied that the constitutional provision forbidding restrictions on the importation of slaves prior to 1808 gave implied powers to pass laws after that date. He further denied that slave trade was necessarily piracy, a term which he contended could only be applied to the violent seizure of free individuals by crews of American ships. Since slavery was legal in equatorial Africa, as well as in the United States, the purchase of Negroes from African owners constituted no change of status which could possibly be called piracy.

Jackson dwelt, in one of his shorter speeches (two hours), on the evidence of the case, particularly concerning the conspiracy.

In his charge the next day Justice Wayne went as far as he properly could to influence the jury for conviction. He discussed the horrors of the overseas voyage, the terrible loss of life, and the moral degradation, quoting missionaries freely. Then he covered the constitutional and legal aspects of the case. He insisted that the act of 1820 was constitutional, that the overseas slave trade had been legally and properly designated piracy, and that the death penalty was a legitimate one.[7]

In the heat of late May in Savannah the jury was kept locked up without food or sleep for thirty hours. Finally, the foreman reported that the jury could not agree. Wayne withdrew a juror and declared a mistrial. The vote was said to be ten to two for acquittal.[8]

Between trials, Jackson and Lamar attended political meetings in which they were on opposite sides. Jackson supported Howell Cobb, who sought the Democratic nomination for president in

1860. One of Cobb's maneuvers was to get the Democratic members of the state legislature to appoint delegates to the national convention pledged to himself and to his platform. When there was complaint about this irregular method of choosing delegates he tried to smooth things over by getting county conventions to elect the same delegates and give them the same instructions as the legislators had voted.

Jackson led Cobb's forces at the Chatham County convention January 25, 1860. Lamar and his friends wanted to embarrass Jackson and Cobb. When Jackson made his motion that the previous action be legitimized, Lamar moved that the motion be tabled and one of his friends offered a substitute. Several people made speeches at the same time. Votes were taken, recounts made, tallies challenged, and a scuffle broke out on the stand. The auditorium was so crowded that a proper count of votes was impossible. The meeting was adjourned and Lamar's group, apparently a majority, left the hall to Jackson's crowd, who elected John Boston chairman and adopted Jackson's resolutions.[9] Similar discord took place in other county conventions.

Thus, Georgia sent two groups of delegates to the Charleston convention. A compromise was offered whereby both delegations would be seated, with each person getting half a vote. This was unacceptable and a floor fight ensued. Although his forces won, Cobb's claim to favorite-son status was wrecked. It became a bit easier for Stephen A. Douglas' platform to be adopted, for the Democratic party to split, and for Abraham Lincoln to win the election. Lamar did not start the Civil War, but he helped remove one more of the possibilities of its being averted.

Lamar and his followers selected May 1, 1860, for their next move. The military companies of Savannah were holding their annual meetings. The town was crowded with strangers and with those politicians who were not at the National Democratic Convention. County jailor Charles W. Stone left his deputy, Peter Luddy, in charge of the prisoners, including Farnum, who had long ago given his parole that he would not try to escape if he could wander freely within the jail. That evening at about seven Farnum came to Luddy and asked to be locked up. He did not want to continue his parole. Luddy put him in his cell and returned to the front of the jail. Somehow it did not occur to Luddy that giving a parole was, in those genteel times, a necessary prelude to an escape attempt. Farnum, an outlander, would probably have flown the coop without formality; his associates were bound by the letter but decidedly not by the spirit of a code of chivalry which they thought extended back a thousand years.

When Luddy got to the front of the jail he was met by seven or eight knights-errant, including Charles Lamar, Mott Middleton, William Hone, and Carey Styles. Somebody said pleasantly, "Peter, old boy, we want the keys." Luddy thought it was a joke but then saw cocked revolvers pointed at him. Someone jumped him; his collar was torn and a pocket ripped off as his assailants grabbed for the keys. They released Farnum and drove him to the Pulaski House, Savannah's leading hotel, where Hone had a room. Farnum was the guest of honor at a party of twenty or thirty gentlemen. There was no effort at concealment.

About nine o'clock United States Attorney Hamilton Couper happened by the hotel and saw what was going on. He soon returned with a deputy marshal, the jailor, and a couple of friends. Hammers were drawn back on revolvers. Couper said that he had come to arrest Farnum. Styles said that no one should lay hands on the captain. Couper asked if they defied the law. Someone suggested that the arrest be postponed until morning, when they gave their promise that Farnum would turn himself in. Badly outnumbered, with no public support, and confident that his adversaries would keep their word, Couper agreed. He had been badly outmaneuvered. Lamar's group had succeeded in making the law look impotent. The return of Farnum was made to look like an act of courtesy rather than obedience to the power of the government.

Next morning Farnum failed to appear. Instead, there was a bond for Farnum with the amount left blank, signed by men worth a million dollars. That did not suit Couper. He wanted Farnum and insisted that the jail breakers keep their promises. That afternoon Farnum appeared; he was ready to put up bail. Couper said that was a matter to be discussed after surrender, not before. Still in keeping with the chivalric code, he said that if the accused pirate thought he had been tricked, he could go back to the hotel and Couper would follow with a posse powerful enough to capture him. Farnum surrendered and was put back in jail. One of the alleged jail-breakers named Daniels dropped dead in the Pulaski Hotel.[10]

Styles wrote a newspaper story of Farnum's jailbreak and subsequent recovery in which Styles made Couper look like a fool, a coward, and no gentleman. According to Styles, Couper was completely overawed at the Pulaski House and begged off with a promise that Farnum would be released on bail upon request. Then

Couper had gone back on his word and clapped Farnum in jail.
Couper replied by sending his version to the *Savannah Daily
Morning News.* Charles Lamar wrote him a note that Styles' story
was "a statement of fact and occurrences." In other words, Couper
was lying. Couper acknowledged receipt of the letter but made
no other comment. Lamar pressed him, asking if Couper were
accusing Lamar of falsehood. They were now on deadly ground.
Lamar obviously wanted a duel. Couper wrote back that if Lamar
adhered to Styles' story he was guilty of falsehood. Lamar challenged. Couper accepted. Other citizens intervened and got both
parties to agree that the whole affair was a misunderstanding of
phraseology.[11] The city calmed down again.

On May 31, 1860, Farnum and Stone, the jailer, were sitting
on the steps on the north side of the jail between two and three
o'clock in the sultry afternoon trying to get a breath of air. There
was a flash and a loud report. Farnum exclaimed, "My God, I'm
shot!" Lightning had struck two nearby pine trees, charring them
for several feet and making a three-inch hole at the foot of one,
but hurting no one. The bolt had come from an almost clear sky.[12]

After Farnum's piracy trial in May, 1860, Lamar, Hone, Middleton, and Styles were indicted by a federal grand jury for "the
rescue of Farnum." At the same time no bills were found against
James Phinizy, Gazaway B. Lamar, Jr. (both first cousins of
Charles), and W. R. Pritchard.

Lamar and his three accomplices pled guilty on May 21 and
were sentenced to thirty days imprisonment and fines of $250.[13]
Although Brown had been kept in the county jail for over a year
and Farnum for seven months, the jail was considered unfit and
unwholesome for use of the local gentry, and they were allowed to
maintain their own quarters above Lamar's office. As Styles remembered it later, they held picnics downriver on Tybee Island
and at Thunderbolt. Styles was even said to have made political
speeches while theoretically in jail.[14]

Challenges to duels were numerous around Savannah that spring.
In addition to the duel between Lamar and Moore and the near
duel between Lamar and Couper, two other encounters threatened.
In one instance Farnum and Jackson were involved. Farnum wanted
to get out of jail long enough to fight Henry Jackson for publishing
the statement that Farnum was trying to sell out his accomplices.
Farnum could not gain his release and Jackson could not prove
his contentions. The other case was a letter from an unknown

congressman to Lamar addressed, "In Jail." Lamar asked Lucius Lamar to find out who it was and challenge him for Charlie.

I am not in jail, and the damned Government has not the power to put and keep me there. I am in my own rooms, over my office, and go home every night, and live like a fighting cock at the expense of the Government; for we notified the Marshal, at the beginning, that unless he furnished us, we would not stay with him, but dissolve all connection that exists or might exist between us. He submitted the same to the Judges, and they told him to supply us. I can whip the Government any time they make the issue, unless they raise a few additional regiments.[15]

Delivering Farnum from jail, taking him to a public party at a leading hotel, defying law enforcement officers, and then returning Farnum after the agreed time were not merely high-spirited pranks. The jury had to be convinced of the continued overwhelming power of the Lamar faction. The town must be kept in a state of excitement so that its prejudices might be felt in court. Most important was the effect on Farnum, a stranger to the community. The ease of his release and the open defiance of law must have made him confident of escape if he were convicted. Further, it was a warning to Farnum that neither prison walls nor Jackson's assurances would save him from vengeance if he betrayed the *Wanderer* conspirators. Farnum never wavered.

IX

Wanderer Is Stolen

AFTER LAMAR bought the *Wanderer* at auction in March, 1859, he went to considerable expense to refurbish her. At $4,001 she was not a bargain; she had taken such a beating on her slave-trading mission and the subsequent four months of neglect in government hands. Prolonged fumigation by smoke and scrubbing with lye and vinegar were necessary to kill teeming colonies of roaches and to eliminate loathsome odors. Missing bulkheads had to be replaced, seams caulked, the whole vessel repainted, and replacement spars, sails, and cordage prepared.

By the time of the grand jury hearings in mid-April, 1859, she was ready for a trial run at sea. Almost immediately sloppily seamanship lost the *Wanderer* her main boom, split several sails, and she had to be towed back to Savannah. The *Wanderer* was no toy for amateur sailors. No sportsman would or could buy her. Realizing that her value as a yacht had been vastly reduced by her reputation as a slaver, Lamar planned a trip to Cuba hoping to sell her there, probably to someone who wanted to run slaves from Africa to Cuba. A June cruise to Havana brought no purchaser. In July, while considering a plan to enter the *Wanderer* in the Chinese coolie trade which the British found so profitable and so clear of legal and presumably moral restrictions, Lamar used the *Wanderer* for short fishing trips with friends.

Toward the end of the summer he brought her back up the river and had her sails put in his warehouse at the cotton press. The Revenue cutter *James C. Dobbins,* which had been tagging along like a chaperon trying to catch her doing something wrong, lay nearby continuing to keep watch. In early October, 1859, the *Wanderer* entered a new career which included theft, piracy, kidnapping, and marooning.[1]

A stranger in Savannah who used the name David Martin said he wanted the speedy *Wanderer* for the fruit trade. Lamar accepted his offer of $20,000 for a three-fourths interest in the vessel.[2] Martin intended to command the vessel himself after the purchase was completed and registry was made out in his name. Until registry had been changed, authority to leave port required Lamar's concurrence. Martin kept failing to meet his promises to pay, but while he evaded Lamar, he talked Lamar's warehouse watchman into letting him as prospective captain remove some of the vessel's gear and put it on board. Lamar was furious when he found this out and he had the *Wanderer* towed away from the pier and anchored in mid-river where it would be harder to sneak equipment from the warehouse. Martin was still unable to make payment.

Lamar was called out of town on a legal matter. He ordered his clerk to press for payment for the ship and implied, but did not direct, that if payment was not made Martin should be evicted.

Court adjourned early. Lamar returned to Savannah on the rainy morning of October 18. Driving along the waterfront he saw no activity on his yacht. Later he was told that provisions had been embarked and that a crew was being assembled; when he went to his warehouse he discovered that sails and spars had been removed. He had not been paid. In the early afternoon he hailed the *Wanderer* but was told Captain Martin was not aboard. He sent a messenger aboard to ask Martin to come to his office. Martin never came. Fearful of Martin's honesty, Lamar went to the home of Custom Collector John Boston. He asked that the revenue cutter be alerted to the possibility that Martin might run away with the *Wanderer* and demanded that the cutter seize his vessel. That very day the cutter had gone to sea, and the custom officer had no other vessel. Lamar went home, determined to take action the first thing next morning.[3]

At daybreak Lamar was greeted with the news that the *Wanderer* had sailed. He hurried to the custom house and, pushing his way through the excited crowd to John Boston, demanded assistance in recovering his vessel. The collector protested that he had no cutter and that hiring a vessel was beyond his authority. Someone came in with news that the *Wanderer* had grounded in the river below the town. Lamar jammed his black beaver hat down on his head and rushed through the bystanders to the Exchange tower.

Puffing and red-faced, he reached the top and sighted his yacht 18 miles downriver, masts naked of sails, ship heeled over at an odd angle, across the stream, obviously aground. The tide was out. There might be time to catch her before she refloated. Lamar came charging down the stairs once more, followed by the idle, the curious, and the energetically helpful. It was whispered that Lamar had staged the theft in order to get the *Wanderer* past port authorities with equipment aboard for another slave-trading venture.

Whether for deception or for honest reasons, Lamar acted with his usual vigor and drive. He ran panting into the custom house, loudly demanding government help. Within an hour he had persuaded Boston to furnish him two officers, had hired at his expense —if the Treasury Department refused payment—a steamboat and had embarked a large armed posse of friends and onlookers. The *Columbus* shoved off at 10:15 A.M. with Lamar aboard. If the *Wanderer* remained stuck, or if winds were adverse to her, they could catch her.

Spectators crowding the Exchange tower saw the *Columbus* make black smoke as she pushed downriver. About 11:30 A.M., before the *Columbus* was halfway to her, the *Wanderer* squared away for sea her sails came out in white clouds as she filled away to the southeast. She had a 10-mile start. By noon she could no longer be seen from the Exchange.

The night before a scene reminiscent of *Treasure Island* had taken place aboard the *Wanderer*.

"The first son of a bitch that goes over the rail, I'll blow his brains out!" Captain Martin bellowed from the galley door of the *Wanderer*. The red light of dying embers from the cook's fire glinted on horse pistols in the captain's fists. His sailors sprang to their feet, knocking ashes from their pipes. That morning rain had interrupted loading the vessel, but the captain had them hard at it ever since, and now—nine o'clock at night—they were still to get no rest, though it was a full week until the vessel was to sail.

"I'll blow the brains out of any man who attempts to leave," Martin rasped. "Lay up to the cabin," he ordered and led the men along the dark, cluttered deck.

The silence was broken only by the bumping splash of a small boat tied astern, A few minutes earlier this boat had brought Captain Martin and two men whose faces the sailors could remember having seen in the shipping agent's office. Their names were William F. Black and Ned Talbot, and before them only a few days earlier the sailors had signed their shipping articles, the seaman's work contract, for a four or five weeks' voyage to Cuba and back for fruit.

Sailors crowded the cabin. Against damask draperies on the port side were about a dozen muskets; lying on the carpet were as many cutlasses. The steward was standing by with champagne, wine, and whiskey. The sailors were ordered to step forward one at a time. Each time a man stepped up, the captain offered him a drink, showed him shipping articles to St. Helena laid out on a cushion of the settee beside William Black, and, with no explanation but a gesture with his pistol, ordered the man to sign. Nobody had a chance to ask whether the St. Helena mentioned was on the Georgia coast near the South Carolina line or was Napoleon's old prison off the African slave coast.

The procedure was for William Black to sign their names. The men touched the pen as he wrote and then made an X where he indicated. Martin watched with his bloodshot good eye, but the open, blind, white eye stared at the men also. The first few, apparently old shipmates of Martin, signed on, then loaded muskets with buckshot. Some of the later men hesitated. When one hung back, Martin thrust a pistol into his ear or chest. All signed. Martin wanted his first mate, Henry Welton, to sign "John Boston" as witness, but Welton refused. The crew was now committed to a voyage of unknown duration, indefinite destination, unknown purpose, on a vessel far from ready for sea.

After the thirteen sailors had signed, Martin called down to the boat and ordered the two hired oarsmen to come up on deck.

"Do you want to go ashore or go ahead with this vessel? Mind, before you speak." With the captain's pistol encouraging them, the oarsmen signed on. Each was offered drinks by the captain, who had several for himself. About now, the shipping agent announced, "Me and Ned will go ashore now."

"No, sir. Not a living soul is going over that rail tonight," the captain barked. "I wouldn't trust my own brother. This ship's going to sea. She's going to sea tonight. You said you'd help; now you've got to."

"But I have a wife and children," objected Ned Talbot.

"I need you for a pilot."

Black asked what he was needed for. "To fight," replied Martin, saying he was going to fight off the revenue cutter if she came up. He gave Black two horse pistols, gave Ned a cutlass and a revolver, and had his henchmen load the two six-pounder carriage guns with grapeshot. Martin and Black had more liquor, and the captain

ordered "all hands on deck" to get underway. The crew began
heaving in on the anchor chain and setting sails.

It was almost midnight. The *Wanderer* was 15 miles upriver
with a fisherman acting as pilot and her captain drunk. Ned was
at the wheel. Martin and Black were swearing and giving more
orders than the crew could carry out. The ship went ahead about
two lengths, then grounded. The makeshift pilot had misjudged
the length of time it would take for the ship to gather way
enough to counteract the strong river current. Martin cursed and
threatened to blow Ned's heart out for treachery; Black said the
grounding was an accident and persuaded the captain to get into
the boat and go for a steamer they heard nearby in the darkness to
ask for a tow. Black got into the boat with him, and they started.
Half way to the steamer, the captain ordered, "Hold on pulling.
Pull back again."

"What for?" Black asked.

"Damn you, you want to get ashore. I know your move."

They were rowed back to the ship. Black went down to the
cabin and passed out. The captain had the mate lay out a kedge
anchor to try to pull the vessel off. This failed. After an hour or
so the tide came in and turned the ship clear around and she floated
free. Martin had the cable to the kedge anchor cut and slipped his
sheet (main) anchor, thus losing two anchors before he even left
Savannah.

With Ned Talbot standing in the bow, Welton steering, and
Martin roaring about what he would do to the revenue cutter if
they encountered her, the *Wanderer* lurched through the clear, cold,
moonless night toward the Atlantic. About 4 or 5 A.M., just before
they got to the mouth of the river, Welton put the wheel over the
opposite way from that ordered and the *Wanderer* ran aground
again. Up came Martin with pistols ready, gesticulating wildly.
Welton swore that he had carried out the order as given. Martin
calmed down a little. He took in sails and had a boat carry an
anchor out six or eight fathoms to windward to keep the vessel from
drifting further ashore.

This commotion woke Black, who joined Talbot and Welton
in downing a couple of bottles of liquor. The captain went into his
cabin to fortify himself, and the crew took a few hours' rest until
the tide would come in. By ten o'clock the *Wanderer* was afloat,
but she lost another anchor and fifteen fathoms of chain in her
haste to get to sea. By eleven-thirty she passed Tybee light. The
yacht was in the open sea, gaining speed under full sail. Captain

Martin had Talbot's boat pulled up close under the stern. Black and Talbot jumped down, and the last Black heard was Martin's voice shouting after him, "Now go to hell. My name is Lincoln Patten, and I'm bound to the coast of Africa for a cargo of niggers, and I don't give a goddam who knows it. Give my respects to the people of Savannah and tell them to kiss my arse."

If the *Wanderer* had been delayed another hour by her second grounding, Martin would have had use for his pistols, muskets, cutlasses, and brass cannon against Lamar's heavily armed friends, creditors, and law officers.

After the *Wanderer* was free of the bottom, Martin harangued the crew in a disjointed speech in which he announced he was going to sell a cargo of seven hundred slaves in Cuba for $650 each. He talked of going to St. Helena's Sound, Georgia, to meet a steamer with twenty tons of rice, twenty men, and clothing for the crew, but he made no motion to carry out this plan. The *Wanderer* stood off Savannah to the southeast for about twelve hours, then headed east. For two or three days Welton kept the log; then Martin tore it up and threw the pieces overboard. Martin began stopping ships to ask for position and to try to buy supplies, for he had neither chronometer, navigation books, charts, nor adequate food or money. On October 23 he bought navigational books and a chart of the Florida coast from the ship *Troy* of Boston for $75. He fired a gun in the direction of the bark *Eliza Brewer* but failed to bring her to. Next day he hailed a sloop and received her position. On the evening of October 28 Martin pursued a brig for three hours, firing grape shot from the *Wanderer's* two little guns, but he failed to stop her. All this time Martin was heading toward the Azores using an old octant to tell the ship's north and south position and trusting to estimates of his course and speed to check his progress to the east. He was also drinking up the liquor at a rapid rate, holding the yacht before the autumn gales under full sail, and terrifying all hands who expected him to snap a mast or drive the vessel under.

When he could not catch a passing ship, Martin would invent elaborate stories that he owned her, or that his friend had a thousand niggers stowed below in her. Meanwhile he had the carpenter paint out *Wanderer* and print in *William*. The real *William* was then in Cuba, about to sail on a voyage which ended when she was captured with 570 slaves on board. When the paint peeled off Martin's sign, he had the carpenter cut letters of metal and nail them to the stern.

After eighteen days the *Wanderer* came in sight of the island of

Flores in the Azores. Martin instructed his mates and six men in the
art of perjury. They were to go to the American consul's office
next day as passengers of the *William* and swear that a sudden
storm had swept away the navigational instruments, charts, most
of the provisions, and almost all the ship's papers. To keep everybody loyal he promised to blow the brains out of anyone who lied
poorly. "God damn you, I want no hesitation about it," he ordered,
and his sailors obeyed. Martin produced old papers falsified to the
effect that his ship was the *William* of Savannah headed for Smyrna,
Turkey, with a cargo of silk. Since the *Wanderer's* previous captain's name was Walker, Martin became Walker instead of Patten,
as he had been since leaving Savannah.

Captain Martin dealt mostly with the British consul, who was
also a ship supplier. The consul's son and Martin worked some kind
of kick-back deal whereby the son received back ashore in a boat
some of the stores. The quantities Martin sought and got were
enormous for a small island to supply and a small vessel to need:
thirty to forty bushels of potatoes, thirty dozen chickens, two large
casks of fish, a butchered pig, several salted beeves, thirty eight casks
of water for a deck load, two or three cords of firewood, an anchor
and fifteen fathoms of chain, twenty blankets, and a number of
casks of liquor. Two Portuguese girls, Anna Felice and Maria Jose,
were enticed aboard with promises of money or matrimony.

During the sixth day in the Azores, while the carpenter was
ashore making chicken coops and Martin was visiting the American
consul to pick up oranges, Martin sensed something wrong, jumped
into his waiting boat, and was hurriedly rowed back to his ship,
giving the boat crew orders to loosen sail as soon as they got aboard.
He ran up to the forecastle and slipped the anchor chain, losing
another anchor and fifteen fathoms of chain. They set sail so fast
they left twenty tons of flour and the carpenter ashore and had in
exchange the Portuguese customs officer and a pilot. Martin
threatened to throw the terrified officer overboard, but he liked the
weatherbeaten old pilot enough to run the vessel back in to leave
the two men off, meanwhile firing the two cannon to attract the carpenter's attention and get him back aboard. The carpenter seems
to have been too busy with his chicken coops to hear the call to
duty; he was left behind while the rest of the crew proceeded toward
Africa.

A few days after leaving Flores Martin, drunk as usual after
dinner, was telling dirty stories and making fun of Welton because
he would not sleep with the women aboard. Martin spent all his

time with them, rarely coming on deck, even when he was supposed to be on watch. When Martin revealed that he intended trading the two women in Africa for eighty to a hundred slaves apiece, Welton exclaimed, "This will never do!"

Martin jerked his head up at this open opposition. He needed Welton on his side. "Give you ten thousand dollars to stick by me," he offered.

"Keep your money. I didn't ship to go pirating and slaving," Welton replied.

Martin cursed and threatened. Welton said he did not care.

"I'll shoot the first man who refuses duty," Martin hissed.

"Well," said Welton levelly, "another man can shoot a pistol off just as well as you can."

They were silent. Martin gulped his liquor. At the door of the cabin he turned, said briefly, "Never mind," and left.

Their disagreements continued. Welton complained, "I had a good ship when I came to Savannah, and all the money I had you borrowed of me, saying you were going on a nice voyage for fruit, and you shanghaied me aboard this vessel, without giving me time to get my clothes, or to write to my wife and family. I have never been slaving, and I never will go. Why didn't you pick out a rogue like yourself, to go mate of the vessel?"

For ten days the quarreling kept up, until the *Wanderer* arrived off Madeira, where Captain Martin, sighting a vessel in the harbor with steam on, decided to wait until nightfall before going in.

Welton came restlessly to the cabin and, seeing there only the second mate and a responsible sailor, said that he did not like the way things were going, concluding, "I wish the steamer were a man-of-war, and would take us."

"Yes," said Second Mate King, "so do I."

Welton looked inquiringly at the sailor, Sommers. He had often wondered whether or not to trust Sommers. This time he asked him, "How many men forward do you think you could trust?"

"Three or four men besides the cook, I guess you could trust."

Welton said, "You keep your eye open."

Martin came below. The two mates went up on deck.

At dark the *Wanderer* started to enter the harbor. The steamer was indeed a man of war. Martin sheered off and continued south for the coast of Africa, saying he would take provisions by force from passing vessels. The first encountered was French, did not understand what the captain wanted, and paid no attention to the guns he was getting ready, but the second came along quite soon after, and by then the guns were ready. Martin hoisted colors as if in distress and asked for provisions. Food being available, battle was averted. Martin had four men launch a boat and went himself for the provisions.

While Martin was on the quarterdeck of the *Jeannie* and his four sailors were lowering a barrel into the boat, Welton was watching from the *Wanderer*. The mate turned to Sommers, "Harry, now is the time—get me two pistols."

The sailor hurried to get two pistols from the rack in the captain's stateroom. Welton ordered the man at the wheel to "put it hard up and run across her stern," sung out for the rest to "hoist the foresail," then got the mainsail set and let her go. Welton laid the pistols down and helped pull on the halyards himself. The *Wanderer* leaped ahead. Then, picking up the pistols again, he called the crew together aft and announced, "I am going to give the vessel up to the authorities of the United States, and I hope you are all willing to."

Captain Martin and his four sailors were left bouncing about in mid-ocean in a small boat. Martin pursued the *Wanderer* for some hours but could not catch her and meantime he lost sight of the *Jeannie*. After a day he was picked up by the French bark *Marguerite,* which took him and his boat to Teneriffe.

With his customary reckless audacity Martin reported his vessel, the *William* of Savannah, her cargo of silk, and $27,000 in gold doubloons stolen from him in mid-ocean. Using the name Captain George D. Walker, he booked passage for himself and four sailors to Liverpool, where he chartered a British vessel for a voyage to Africa for palm oil. They also let it be known they were looking for investors and crewmen for a combination slave-trade and piracy voyage.[4] Being his usual convincing self, Martin soon had a good number of men and supplies obtained before port authorities arrested him. The United States consul in Liverpool sent Martin home as a distressed seaman.[5]

Martin had more nerve and luck than skill. He liked to crowd on all possible canvas even in fairly strong winds and to pass the bottle to the apprehensive watch. The *Wanderer* was one of the fastest vessels of her time, but Martin had not handled her properly. He had a good working knowledge of seamanship, but he was brutal in his application of it. On the second day out, coming through the wind in a careless manner, he jibed, unshipping the main boom and splitting the brand new mainsail. Another time he sprung the tall foremast by placing too great a strain on it in a strong breeze.

Again, he broke the jibboom when getting underway. In the two weeks it took to reach the Azores, Martin had wrecked most of the delicate apparatus that made the *Wanderer* the marvelous vessel she was. He also deprived himself of the blinding speed which might have made a successful slaving voyage possible. Worse still, he had destroyed the confidence of his officers and men in him.

Martin had several other names besides Walker and Patten. Since the real Captain Patten objected that he had been at home in Maine for some time, the newspapers soon identified Martin as Captain Gilman Dresser of Harpswell, Maine, who was said to have been a fine, upright seaman until a bale of cotton fell on his head in New Orleans, addled his brain, and very likely kept him from being quite so upright. Dresser's wife reported the real Dresser at sea in command of a large vessel en route from Portland to New Orleans. Martin was also represented as an illegitimate Welshman turned Australian, named Archibald, who went around causing mutinies and murdering people in the South Pacific. Old Australian hands wrote to the paper and said it had been duped; the stories about Archibald had geographical and historical errors that made them implausible. One Welshman suggested that the paper "drop the leek and try the thistle.[6] Martin, Walker, Patten, Dresser, or Archibald, Yankee, Aussie, Scot, or Welshman, whoever he might be, Charles Lamar swore that he was a thief. He had stolen the *Wanderer* and had run away with her. The charge of the United States versus David S. Martin alias James F. Patten, alias Dresser, alias Walker, resulted in an indictment by the grand jury of the United States circuit court for the district of Georgia on November 24, 1860.[7]

Martin was arrested sometime between November, 1860, and June, 1861. His trial took place in November, 1861, in one of several cases tried before Confederate States courts rather than in the individual state courts. The case was titled *United States* v. *David S. Martin* and was held in the district court of the Confederate States, southern district of Georgia. Judge Nicoll, who had resigned as United States district judge, had been appointed Confederate States attorney for the district, and Edward J. Harden was judge. Upon Martin's plea of not guilty, Nicoll responded, "the United States say he is guilty and will prove him so." At first a mistrial was declared after the jury deliberated three hours. A new trial was ordered, but Charles Lamar failed to report as a witness. Cited for contempt, he testified; Martin was found guilty and sentenced on February 18, 1862, to five years' imprisonment and costs.[8] Martin was placed in the Chatham County jail and then moved to the state prison in Milledgeville some time before March, 1864. He apparently remained in prison there until the fall of the Confederacy.[9] Martin submitted a petition for pardon to President Jefferson Davis in early 1864, protesting that he had violated no Confederate law except a general *ex post facto* one continuing United States laws in effect in the Confederacy. Attorney General George Davis wrote his superior that Martin had failed to use the unconstitutionality of the law as a defense during his trial and hence his plea was too late to be considered. He enclosed a copy of Martin's unsatisfactory prison record and doubted validity of some of the signatures on the petition for pardon. President Davis denied the pardon.[10]

First Mate Henry Welton brought the *Wanderer* in to Boston on Christmas Eve, 1859, and turned her over to the customs authorities. Welton and the rest of the crew claimed that they had signed on for a cruise to Matanzas, Cuba, for a cargo of fruit and had no idea Martin was going to take the *Wanderer* on a slaving voyage. This contention was and is hard to believe, since most of the men had signed on the notorious slaver at extraordinarily high wages several days before she sailed and had loaded ammunition, food, and equipment at night at a fairly remote anchorage.

Welton and the crew sued for their wages and also for salvage money. Judge Sprague, as an admiralty court, considered these claims at the same time he considered condemnation proceedings against the *Wanderer* for having been fitted out as a slaver in violation of the act of April 20, 1818. The principal point in contention was whether Charles Lamar, as owner, was responsible for the actions of Martin, since it was clear that Martin had made preparations for and sailed upon a slaving expedition. The court ruled that, even if Martin sailed on a slaving voyage without Lamar's authority, once Martin had been properly placed in command, Lamar was legally responsible for the actions of his craft. Sprague used as an analogy the liability of an ocean liner to forfeiture if one of her crew were convicted of smuggling goods worth as little as $400. Sprague said that this harsh feature of the law was designed to make owners careful in the selection and supervision of their captains.

Lamar's case rested upon establishing that Martin had deceived him from the outset but it was not very convincing. Martin had loaded stores alongside Lamar's own pier in broad daylight with hundreds of persons watching. No effort was made to halt loading or to evict the captain. After the *Wanderer* hired numbers of sailors at high rates of pay and was hauled out into the river, the revenue cutter took that particular time to put to sea. At the same time Lamar left town. When Lamar returned he spent a day talking about stopping the vessel from sailing but did not hire a steamer until he saw from the top of the tower that the *Wanderer* was at the mouth of the river. Only then did he get revenue officers and armed friends aboard a steamer and make a show of pursuing the *Wanderer*. Lamar's record and reputation in the slave trade must have told heavily against him in Boston and was probably the deciding factor.

The *Wanderer* was declared forfeited, the money from her sale to be used to pay wages of her crew with the exception of Welton, who was presumed to have known Martin's intention. Salvage money was not allowed the crew, since she had not been saved from forfeiture, her only danger.[11]

By October, 1860, Gazaway Bugg Lamar claimed ownership of the yacht as payment of a debt and appealed the decision to condemn her. Meanwhile, the vessel was released to him on $5,000 bond. John A. Andrew and Albert G. Browne, Jr., who had represented Charles Lamar withdrew from the case; they did not wish to be associated with a slave-trading case.[12] Gazaway Lamar then obtained the services of Caleb Cushing, former attorney general of the United States and distinguished diplomat, who was fighting to reunite his New England section of the Democratic party with the rebellious Southern faction.[13] Cushing continued his appeals until June 28, 1862, when the United States circuit court in Boston finally decided against the Lamars in a wartime situation obviously prejudiced toward the Lamars.

X

Conclusion

THE CIVIL WAR brought an end to the slave trade and freedom to the *Wanderer's* cargo. It brought seizure to the *Wanderer* and service as a Union gunboat. It brought modest fame as a Union general to the adventurer Farnum. It brought a Confederate military career and death to Charles Lamar, who had been such a hot secessionist he feared that Lincoln would be defeated and secession would become impossible.

During the tense period between Lincoln's election and the outbreak of war, the Lamars put up bond while appealing the *Wanderer's* condemnation and then refurbished their yacht. By December, 1860, Charles Lamar reasserted ownership in her and had sent her to Cuba in charge of Nelson Trowbridge. There Trowbridge sold her to Thomas J. Smith for $15,000, but in a secret clause Charles Lamar retained half ownership and Smith agreed to pay Lamar "one fourth of the profits arising from any or all enterprises in which she may be engaged."[1]

Perhaps the *Wanderer* was expected to become a slaver or a blockade-runner, but more probably Lamar wanted to make her a privateer. Subsequently Lamar bought the seized slaver *Bonita* for this purpose, and Corrie applied for a letter of marque and reprisal.[2] A week before Fort Sumter was fired upon, the *Wanderer* showed up at Key West, and six weeks later Lieutenant T. A. Craven seized her, writing to the United States secretary of the navy that since she would make such a good privateer for the Confederates he captured her before she could do any harm.[3]

Secretary Gideon Welles incorporated the *Wanderer* into the

United States Navy without legal proceedings of any kind, manned her with naval officers and men, and even referred to her as *U.S.S. Wanderer* although there was no known formal commissioning.

Ironically, the *Wanderer's* principal service to the Union was as a water-carrier; her huge tank capacity made it possible for converted steamers to remain on blockading stations instead of withdrawing to replenish water. She also acted as dispatch vessel, blockading vessel, and gunboat. Armed with a 20-pound Parrot rifle and for a while with a pair of 24-pounder Dahlgren howitzers, she is credited with capturing the sloops *Belle, Ranger,* and *Anna B* in addition to destroying Confederate salt works between Pensacola and St. Andrews Bay.[4] On November 30, 1861, she seized the British schooner *Telegraph* off the Bahamas; a minor diplomatic crisis developed when a British sailor was kept handcuffed for three days for cursing his captors.[5] The news of this encounter arrived in England about the same time as word of the affair of the *Trent* and added to the seriousness of the situation.

In May, 1863, Craven's seizure was considered in a Philadelphia court, and the *Wanderer* was declared a legal prize. The navy bought her for $1,125 and at last officially incorporated her in the United States Navy, although by now steamers had replaced most sailing ships on naval duty.[6] On June 28, 1865, she was sold at public auction in Key West to the firm of Packer and Watson for $2,760.[7] Her history now becomes obscure. She is said to have been sold to Captain Josiah Rowe of Rockland, Maine, and rebuilt for $7,000 just to save her hull lines.[8] Rowe is supposed to have damaged her while entering St. Thomas, Virgin Islands, and to have repaired and sold her to I. L. Snow and Company, who took eight feet off her masts and continued her in trade.[9]

After the war, Gazaway B. Lamar tried to recover his and his late son's property, including the *Wanderer,* even addressing a pamphlet to ex-President Andrew Johnson in 1869.[10] Apparently this effort failed, for that same year the *Wanderer* was registered by S. S. Scattergood of Philadelphia for the West Indian fruit trade. She was grounded once off Cape Henry and finally lost on Cape Maisi, Cuba, on January 21, 1871.[11]

The voyage of the *Wanderer* which ended at Jekyll Island in 1858 was undoubtedly a financial success for its share-holders, even when large lawyers' fees and probable bribes were subtracted. Whether the venture over the entire period 1857-1860 was profitable is another matter; the probability is that any net gain was small.

Ideologically, the situation was similar. The fact that not a single crewman or investor was convicted, that the condemned yacht was repurchased for a nominal sum, and that the government was unable to maintain custody of even one of the *Wanderer's* slave cargo resulted in a short-term victory for the pro-slave-trade group. On the other hand, Southern leaders, seeking to remove divisive influences from their region on the eve of the 1860 election, rejected the extreme position of Lamar, Spratt, and Gaulden. Slave trade by American-owned ships to Cuba from Africa continued to be attempted on a large scale, but the challenge to laws against importations into the United States diminished to the frustrated voice of Spratt, who continued to advocate his pet measure to the Confederate congress.

The 409 Negroes brought by the *Wanderer* lived out their lives in a variety of ways: some died soon after the landing; others were long in regaining their strength, a galling expense to their owners; many never strayed far from where they were first settled. In 1908, 1930, and 1940, an anthropologist, a local historian, and a group of WPA writers interviewed ex-slaves in the coastal areas of South Carolina and Georgia.[12] Several Negroes claimed to have come to the United States in the *Wanderer* or to have heard Africans tell the story of their voyage. Tom Floyd lived on St. Simons Island across the sound from Jekyll Island. His sister, Clementine (also called "Steamboat") had belonged to the Dubignon family and still lived on their place. A third had lived all his life on the Tillman plantation in Edgefield. Like many old people, they tended to remember things that never happened or which happened to someone else. The thing that set them apart from their fellows was the claim of landing on the lonely beach of Jekyll Island in November, 1858.

Until the Civil War, newspapers followed the destinies of *Wanderer* Negroes who were discovered in all the states of the lower South. Twenty were allegedly found on a Colorado River plantation in Texas. Bedford Forrest's slave-trading company in Memphis was supposed to have offered six for sale. A free Negro barber in Augusta, Georgia, was said to own one.

The fact that the *Wanderer's* Negroes are frequently identified with their ship in newspapers and private correspondence whereas no other sizable group of Negroes is so related to a ship supports the belief that there was no other large-scale importation of African slaves to the United States in the 1850's. The only other vessel whose name occurs is the *Clotilda*, which made a disastrously fatal

attempt to land slaves in Mobile Bay in 1859. Reports from marshals, revenue cutters, collectors of customs, and federal secret
agents agreed: no additional large-scale landings had occurred.
Numerous rumors were investigated, but they were either un-
founded, hoaxes to make Yankees look silly, or else the reported
Africans proved to be of the *Wanderer's* cargo.[13]

Partly as a result of the *Wanderer's* landing, the Buchanan administration strengthened the African squadron by adding steamers
of war and by permitting closer co-operation with the British.

While it is undoubtedly true that individuals or small numbers
were smuggled in from the West Indies, especially Cuba, it is unlikely that the number was great. An African field hand in Cuba
was worth about $600 in 1859-1860. Why should a smuggler risk
his money and perhaps his life bringing contraband into the United
States for a maximum net gain of a few hundred dollars? Lamar's
group had entered the slave trade mainly as a matter of principle.
They had shown that Africans could be brought in. They had not
proved the overseas slave trade to the United States worthwhile as
a continuous endeavor, and they found only lukewarm support
among fellow Southerners. Lamar's venture, like John Brown's raid,
was far more important in arousing suspicion and resentment by
those opposed to it than in accomplishing the purposes intended by
its leaders.

Appendix I

Section 5. If any citizen of the United States, being of the crew or ship's company of any foreign ship or vessel engaged in the slave-trade, or any person whatever, being of the crew or ship's company of any ship or vessel, owned wholly or in part, or navigated for or in behalf of any citizen or citizens of the United States, shall forcibly confine or detain, or aid and abet in forcibly confining or detaining, on board such ship or vessel, any negro or mulatto, not held to service by the laws of either of the states or territories of the United States, with intent to make such negro or mulatto a slave, or shall, on board any such ship or vessel, offer or attempt to sell, as a slave, any negro or mulatto not held to service as aforesaid, or shall, on the high seas, or anywhere on tide-water, transfer or deliver over, to any other ship or vessel, any negro or mulatto not held to service as aforesaid, with intent to make such negro or mulatto a slave, or shall land, or deliver on shore, from on board any such ship or vessel, any such negro or mulatto, with intent to make sale of, or having previously sold, such negro or mulatto as a slave, such citizen or person shall be adjudged a pirate; and on conviction thereof before the circuit court of the United States for the district wherein he shall be brought or found, shall suffer death.

Appendix II

Section 6. And be it further enacted, That if any person or persons whatsoever shall, from and after the passing of this act, bring within the jurisdiction of the United States, in any manner whatsoever, any negro, mulatto, or person of colour, from any foreign kingdom, place, or country, or from sea, or shall hold, sell, or otherwise dispose of, any such negro, mulatto, or person of colour, so brought in, as a slave, or to be held to service or labour, or be in any wise aiding or abetting therein, every person so offending shall, on conviction thereof by due course of law, forfeit and pay, for every such offence, a sum not exceeding ten thousand nor less than one thousand dollars, one moiety to the use of the United States, and the other to the use of the person or persons who shall sue for such forfeiture, and prosecute the same to effect; and, moreover, shall suffer imprisonment, for a term not exceeding seven years nor less than three years.

Section 7. And be it further enacted, That if any person or persons whatsoever shall hold, purchase, sell, or otherwise dispose of, any negro, mulatto, or person of colour, for a slave or to be held to service or labour, who shall have been imported or brought, in any way, from any foreign kingdom, place, or country, or from the dominions of any foreign state immediately adjoining to the United States, into any port or place within the jurisdiction of the United States, from and after the passing of this act, every person so offending, and every person aiding or abetting therein, shall severally forfeit and pay, for every negro, mulatto, or person of colour, so held, purchased, sold, or disposed of, one thousand dollars, one moiety to the use of the United States, and the other to the use of the person or persons who may sue for such forfeiture, and prosecute the same to effect, and to stand committed until the said forfeiture be paid: Provided, That the aforesaid forfeiture shall not extend to the seller or purchaser of any negro, mulatto, or person of colour, who may be sold or disposed of in virtue of any regulations which have been heretofore, or shall hereafter be, lawfully made by any legislature of any state or territory in pursuance of this act and the constitution of the United States.

Notes

Chapter One

1. Rebecca Lamar McLeod, "The Loss of the Steamer *Pulaski*," *Georgia Historical Quarterly*, III (1919), 20.
2. Gazaway B. Lamar Account Book, Lamar Papers, University of Georgia. Hereinafter cited as G. B. Lamar Papers.
3. Anonymous, "A Slave-Trader's Letter-Book," *North American Review*, CLXLIII (1886), 449. Hereinafter cited as "Letterbook."
4. John B. Lamar to Mary Ann Cobb, June 12, 1858, Howell Cobb Papers, University of Georgia. Hereinafter cited as Cobb Papers.
5. Oct. 16, 1858, *ibid.*
6. Telegram, Howell Cobb to John Boston, July 16, 1857, Cobb Papers, Georgia Department of Archives and History; *Savannah Daily Morning News*, July 18, 1857.
7. Consular Form No. 6, Aug. 16, 1857, Consular Letters, Funchal, National Archives; "Letterbook," pp. 450-51.
8. "Letterbook," p. 452.
9. John G. Willis to Lewis Cass, Nov. 19, 1859, Consular Letters, St. Paul de Loando, National Archives.
10. Telegram, Secretary of Interior to Collector of Customs, New Orleans, March 1, 1858, Miscellaneous Letters to Secretary of Interior, National Archives (Microcopy 160, Roll 4).
11. 36th Cong., 2nd Sess., H. Executive Docu. No. 7, pp. 201, 632.
12. Admiralty Journal, Sept. 8, 1958, United States District Court, Charleston, Oct. 1857 to Feb. 1861, Federal Records Center, East Point, Ga.
13. Charles A. L. Lamar, *The Reply of C. A. L. Lamar of Savannah, Georgia, to the Letter of Hon. Howell Cobb, Secretary of Treasury of the United States, Refusing a Clearance to the Ship Richard Cobden* (Charleston, 1858), p. 1 (pamphlet).
14. *Ibid.*
15. *Ibid.*, p. 2.
16. *Ibid.*, p. 6.
17. Register of Vessels, Dec. 16, 1854 (cancelled June 28, 1859), New York, Treasury Department Records, National Archives.

Chapter Two

1. Enrollment of the *Wanderer*, Aug. 4, 1857, National Archives; Register of the *Wanderer*, June 26, 1858, *Wanderer* Folder, Slave Papers, Manuscript Division, Library of Congress. Hereinafter cited as *Wanderer* Folder.
2. *The Spirit of the Times*, XXVIII (1858), 9.

3. Corrie was a lobbyist in Washington, D. C. Engaging and affable, he was so effective that a British consul considered him more powerful than the whole South Carolina congressional delegation. Corrie boasted that he knew the price of every congressman in Washington. Laura A. White, "The United States in the 1850's As Seen by British Consuls," *Mississippii Valley Historical Review,* XIX (1933), 525.

4. Warren S. Howard, *American Slavers and the Federal Law* (Los Angeles and Berkeley, 1963), pp. 250-51.

5. *Ibid.,* pp. 155-64.

6. Crew List, *Wanderer* Folder. Brown's name does not appear.

7. Joseph K. Menn, *The Large Slaveholders of Louisiana, 1860* (New Orleans, 1964), pp. 255-56, 310-11; *New York Herald,* June 8, 1860.

8. *New York Sun,* June 9, 1858; *New York Times,* June 11, 12, 1858; *New York Herald,* Dec. 13, 1858.

9. Feb. 5, 1859.

10. *New York Times,* July 8, 1858.

11. *Washington National Intelligencer,* Jan. 13, 1859, quoting *Savannah Republican,* Jan. 10, 1859.

12. Protection for J. Egbert Farnum dated July 3, 1858, *Wanderer* Folder; *Savannah Daily Morning News,* Nov. 19, 1859.

13. Log of the *Wanderer,* Special Collections, Emory University.

14. Letter dated Oct. 19, 1858, from "Our Naval Correspondent" in *New York Herald,* Feb. 7, 1859.

15. *New York Times,* Dec. 18, 1858.

16. Commodore Charles Wise, RN, to Secretary of the Admiralty, Oct. 28, 1858, ADM 1/5694, Public Record Office.

17. Lewis Cass to George M. Dallas, Dec. 22, 1858, 36th Cong., 2nd Sess., H. Exec. Doc. 7, 289.

18. *New York Herald,* Dec. 15, 1858.

19. Conover to Totten, Oct. 7, 1858, and Conover to Secretary of Navy, Oct. 9, 1858, Letters Received by Secretary of Navy from Commanding Officers of Squadrons, National Archives.

20. Totten to Conover, Dec. 10, 1858, *ibid.*

21. Conover to Secretary of Navy, Dec. 13, 1858, *ibid.*

Chapter Three

1. Commodore Wise to Admiralty, Oct. 28, 1858, ADM 1/5694, Public Record Office; Commodore Inman's Instructions to African Squadron, Sept. 3, 1859, Letters Received by Secretary of the Navy from Commanding Officers of Squadrons, National Archives.

2. McBlair to Conover, Oct. 9, 1857, Letters Received by the Secretary of the Navy from Commanding Officers of Squadrons, National Archives; Willis to Cass, Jan. 26, 1859, Consular Letters, St. Paul de Loando, National Archives.

3. Wise to Admiralty, Oct. 28, 1858, ADM 1/5694, Public Record Office; Rear Admiral John W. Grey, RN, to Inman, March 21, 1859, Letters Received by Secretary of the Navy from Commanding Officers of Squadrons, National Archives.

4. *Ibid.*

5. *Ibid.*

6. Log of the *Wanderer,* Special Collections, Emory University.

7. Letter from *U.S.S. Vincennes,* Oct. 1, 1858, in *New York Herald,* Dec. 15, 1858.

8. Conover to Totten, Oct. 7, 1858, Letters Received by Secretary of the Navy from Commanding Officers of Squadrons, National Archives.

9. Totten to Conover, Dec. 10, 1858, *ibid.*

10. Log of *U.S.S. Vincennes,* National Archives.

11. Conover to Secretary of the Navy, Dec. 13, 1858, Letters Received by Secretary of the Navy from Commanding Officers of Squadrons, National Archives.

Chapter Four

1. The modern spelling is Jekyll.
2. Nov. 23, 1858.
3. *Savannah Daily Morning News,* Nov. 16, 1859.
4. *Ibid.,* Nov. 18, 1859.
5. *Ibid.*
6. *Ibid.,* Nov. 21, 1859; *Wanderer* Folder.
7. *Washington National Intelligencer,* Jan. 4, 1859.
8. *Ibid.; Savanah Daily Morning News,* Nov. 17, 1859; *New York Herald,* Jan. 3, 1859.
9. At the time he was interested in importing slaves, Tucker was a member of the Savannah city council and a director of the Mechanics Savings Bank. He had been an officer in the Republican Blues, a militia company. In 1857 he had bought Drakies Plantation, which he mortgaged heavily with Captain

Dickerson as surety for the loan. He owned about two hundred Negroes, some of whom he hired out.
10. *New York Herald,* Jan. 3, 1859.
11. *Washington National Intelligencer,* Jan. 4, 1859.
12. *New York Herald,* Dec. 25, 1858.
13. *Savannah Daily Morning News,* Nov. 19, 1859.
14. *Ibid.,* Sept. 1, 1858.
15. *Ibid.,* Nov. 19, 1859.
16. *Ibid.,* Nov. 18, 1859.
17. Laura A. White, "The South in the 1850's as Seen by British Consuls," *Journal of Southern History,* X (1935), 38.
18. *New York Herald,* Feb. 7, 1859.
19. Quoted in *Washington National Intelligencer,* Jan. 13, 1859.
20. Quoted in *Savannah Daily Morning News,* Dec. 17, 1858.

Chapter Five

1. Woodford Mabry to Joseph Ganahl, Dec. 8, 1858, Letters Received by Office United States Attorney, National Archives.
2. *Savannah Daily Morning News,* Nov. 19, 1859.
3. Joseph Ganahl to Junius Hillyer, Dec. 15, 1858, Letters Received by Office United States Attorney, National Archives.
4. *Savannah Daily Morning News,* Nov. 18, 1859; *New York Herald,* Jan. 5, 1859.
5. Joseph Ganahl to Charles S. Henry, Dec. 14, 1858, and several undated memoranda, Records of United States Circuit Court, Savannah, Federal Records Center, East Point, Ga.
6. Joseph Ganahl to Woodford Mabry, Dec. 13, 1858, Letters Received by Office United States Attorney, National Archives.
7. Junius Hillyer to Joseph Ganahl, Dec. 21, 1858, Solicitor of Treasury Letters, *ibid.*
8. *Savannah Daily Morning News,* Nov. 18, 1859.

9. Joseph Ganahl to Jeremiah S. Black, Dec. 25, 1858, Letters Received by Office of United States Attorney, National Archives.
10. *Savannah Daily Morning News,* Dec. 29, 1858.
11. Joseph Ganahl to Jeremiah S. Black, Dec. 28, 1858, Letters Received by Office of United States Attorney, National Archives.
12. *Savannah Daily Morning News,* Dec. 29, 1858, and Nov. 18, 1859.
13. *New York Times,* Dec. 13, 1858; *Washington National Intelligencer,* Dec. 16, 1858.
14. 35th Cong. 2nd Sess., S. Exec. Doc. 7, p. 8.
15. For extended discussion of this problem, see Warren S. Howard, *American Slavers and the Federal Law* (Berkeley, 1963).
16. D. H. Hamilton to Jacob Thompson, Dec. 30, 1858; Thompson to Hamilton, Dec. 31, 1858; Hamilton to William Porcher Miles, Jan. 28, 1859; Miles to Thompson, April 17, 1859; all in Miscellane-

ous Letters to Secretary of Interior, National Archives (Microcopy 160, Roll 4).

17. Commissioner Henry had been born in Albany, N. Y., in 1797, but he had come to Georgia after his graduation from Columbia College. He was an alderman of Savannah in 1834, a member of the state legislature, and judge of the Superior Court in 1837. During the Civil War he was clerk of the Confederate States circuit court. He died in 1864.

18. *Savannah Daily Morning News,* Dec. 28, 1858, to Jan. 4, 1859, *passim;* Charles S. Henry to Daniel H. Stewart (warrant for arrest)

Jan. 11, 1859, Records of United States Circuit Court, Savannah, Federal Records Center, East Point, Ga.

19. *The United States* v. *The Yacht "Wanderer,"* Admiralty Minutes, United States District Court, 1834-1870, Federal Records Center, East Point, Ga.

20. C. A. L. Lamar to G. B. Lamar, Jan. 14, 1859, Lamar Papers, Mrs. Albert Howell Collection, Emory University. Hereinafter cited as C. A. L. Lamar Papers.

21. Charles S. Henry to Secretary of Treasury, April 23, 1859, Solicitor of Treasury Letters, National Archives.

Chapter Six

1. Quoted in *New York Times,* Jan. 12, 1859.

2. *Savannah Daily Morning News,* March 12 to April 22, 1859, *passim,* Nov. 19, 1859; Manuscript Records of Circuit Court, Savannah, Federal Records Center, East Point, Ga.

3. *New York Times,* April 15, 22, 1859.

4. C. A. L. Lamar to G. B. Lamar, Jan. 14, 1859, C. A. L. Lamar Papers.

5. C. A. L. Lamar to G. B. Lamar, Jan. 17, 1859, *ibid.;* George W. Lamar to G. B. Lamar, Jan. 26, 1859, G. B. Lamar Papers.

6. *Savannah Daily Morning News,* Nov. 16 and 18, 1859; *New York Tribune,* March 23, 1859.

7. Minutes of Sixth Circuit Court, Savannah, Federal Record Center, East Point, Ga.

8. *Ibid.; Savannah Daily Morning* Jan. 17, 1859, C. A. L. Lamar Papers.

9. Henry R. Jackson to Howell Cobb, Jan. 29, 1859, Cobb Papers.

10. *Savannah Daily Morning News,* Nov. 18, 1859.

11. *Ibid.,* March 14, Nov. 18, 1859; *New York Times,* March 5, 12, 1859.

12. *Savannah Daily Morning News,* May 29, 1860.

13. *New York Times,* March 21, 1859.

14. *Savannah Daily Morning News,* March 29, 30, 1859; *New York Times,* April 1, 4, 1859; *New York Tribune,* March 21, April 21, 1859.

15. *New York Times,* March 22, 1859.

16. "Letterbook," pp. 457-58.

17. *New York Tribune,* April 1, 1859.

18. *The U. S.* v. *The Yacht "Wanderer,"* Admiralty Minutes, U. S. District Court, Savannah, 1834-1870, Federal Records Center, East Point, Ga.; Hillyer to Samuel Ingham, July 23, 1859, Letters Written File, Solicitor of Treasury, National Archives.

19. *New York Herald,* March 23, 28, 29, April 14, June 27, 1859; *Savannah Daily Morning News,* March 28, April 9, May 30, Aug. 27, 1859; *New York Times,* June 4, 1859.

20. Minutes, U. S. District Court, Charleston, Sept. 18, 1859-Nov., 1860, Federal Records Center, East Point, Ga.; *Washington Daily Intelligencer,* Jan. 18, 1859.

21. Minutes, U. S. District Court, Charleston, March 14, 19, 1859, Federal Records Center, East Point, Ga.; *Savannah Daily Morn-*

ing News, April 20, 1859; *Washington National Intelligencer,* May 17, 1859.

22. *Savannah Daily Morning News,* May 25, 1859.
23. *Ibid.*

24. *Ibid.,* Sept. 9, 1858.
25. *Ibid.,* April 16, 18, 20, 1859; *New York Times,* April 18, 1859.
26. *Savannah Daily Morning News,* June 1, 1859.
27. *Ibid.,* Nov. 2, 1859.

Chapter Seven

1. The *U. S.* v. *The Yacht "Wanderer,"* Admiralty Minutes, U. S. District Court, Savannah, 1834-1870, Federal Records Center, East Point, Ga.
2. Quoted in part in Appendix I.
3. J. M. Spullock to Junius Hillyer, Nov. 27, 1860, enclosed in Junius Hillyer to Jacob Thompson, Dec. 18, 1860, Letters Written, Solicitor of Treasury, National Archives.
4. *The Federal Cases, Comprising Cases Argued and Determined in the Circuit and District Courts of United States* (St. Paul, 1894-97), XXIX, Case 18269a. Hereinafter cited as *Federal Cases.*
5. Minutes of Circuit Court, Savannah, 1857-1860, Federal Records Center, East Point, Ga., p. 196. Hereinafter cited as Circuit Court Minutes, Savannah.
6. Quoted in part in Appendix II.
7. Henry R. Jackson to [Howell Cobb?], Nov. 26, 1859, Cobb Papers.

8. Henry R. Jackson, *The Wanderer Case . . . (Atlanta,* [ca. 1891]) pp. 42-43.
9. *Augusta Daily Constitutionalist,* Dec. 30, 1859; *Savannah Daily Morning News,* April 10, 1860.
10. *Savannah Daily Morning News,* May 15, 17, 1860.
11. *U. S.* v. *C. A. L. Lamar,* Circuit Court Records, Savannah, Federal Records Center, East Point, Ga.; *U. S.* v. *R. F. Aiken, R. L. Mott, Henry Dubignon, John F. Tucker,* ibid.
12. Circuit Court Minutes, Savannah, p. 316.
13. *Savannah Republican,* quoted in *Charleston Courier,* May 30, 1860.
14. Alexander A. Lawrence, *James Moore Wayne, Southern Unionist* (Chapel Hill, 1943), p. 166.
15. *Federal Cases,* XXV, 658-69.
16. *Charleston Mercury,* April 19, 1860.
17. *Charleston Courier,* June 6, 1860.
18. Henry R. Jackson to Howell Cobb, April 5, 1860, Cobb Papers.

Chapter Eight

1. Henry R. Jackson, *The Wanderer Case . . .* (Atlanta, [ca. 1891]).
2. *Savannah Daily Morning News,* Aug. 30, 1858.
3. *Ibid.,* Dec. 15, 1858.
4. *New York Times,* Jan. 26, 1859.
5. Claim of Lucien Peyton, April 24, 1860, Letters Received by Secretary of Interior, National Archives.
6. *Charleston Courier,* May 25 and 26, 1860; undated newspaper clipping in possession of Mrs. Albert Howell of Atlanta, Ga.
7. *Savannah Daily Morning News,* May 10, 1860.

8. *Ibid,* May 26, 1860.
9. *Ibid.,* Jan. 25, 1860; *Augusta Daily Constitutionalist,* Jan. 28, 1860.
10. *Charleston Courier,* May 3, 5, 1860; *Charleston Mercury,* May 4, 1860 (copied from *Savannah Republican,* May 3, 1860); *New York Daily Tribune,* May 4, 1860; *New York Herald,* May 12, 1860; *New York Times,* May 7, 8, 1860.
11. Hamilton Couper to James M. Couper, July 22, 1860, in possession of Miss Ann Couper, Atlanta, Ga.

12. *Augusta Daily Constitutionalist,* June 1, 1860.
13. Minutes of Circuit Court of Georgia, 1857-1860, Federal Records Center, East Point, Ga.
14. *Charleston Courier,* June 2, 1860; manuscript biography of Carey W. Styles, Styles Papers, Emory University.
15. "Letterbook," p. 460.

Chapter Nine

1. Unless otherwise stated, facts in this chapter are based upon testimony in the pamphlet *The United States by Information v. the Schooner Wanderer and Cargo* (Boston, 1860).
2. *Federal Cases,* XXIX, 150.
3. *Savannah Daily Morning News,* Oct. 23, 1859.
4. *New York Times,* Feb. 20, 1860.
5. Sarah A. Wallace and Frances E. Gillespie (eds.), *The Journal of Benjamin Moran, 1857-65* (Chicago, 1948), I. 616.
6. Martin's voyage and his maze of aliases were widely reported in newspapers. Some of the reports are *New York Herald,* Nov. 25, 1859, Jan. 4, 16, 1860; *Charleston Courier,* Jan. 5, 6, 7, 11, 17, 21, 25, 1860; *Washington National Intelligencer,* Dec. 29, 1859, Jan. 24, 1860; *New York Times,* Dec. 26, 27, 29, 1859, Feb. 10, 1860; *Boston Daily Evening Transcript,* Dec. 29, 1859.
7. Records of Circuit Court, Savannah, Federal Records Center, East Point, Ga.
8. Minutes of Confederate District Court, Southern Georgia, *ibid.*
9. William M. Robinson, Jr., *Justice in Grey* (Cambridge, 1941), pp. 238-39; Warren Grice, "The Confederate States Court," *Georgia Historical Quarterly,* IX (1925), 147.
10. Rembert W. Patrick (ed.), *The Opinions of the Confederate Attorneys General, 1861-1865* (Buffalo, 1950), p. 379.
11. *Federal Cases,* XXIX, 150.
12. John A. Andrews to Caleb Cushing, Oct. 30, 1860, Caleb Cushing Legal File, Manuscript Division, Library of Congress.
13. G. B. Lamar to Caleb Cushing, Oct. 26, 1860, *ibid.*

Chapter Ten

1. Agreement between N. C. Trowbridge and T. J. Smith, Dec. 12, 1860, G. B. Lamar Papers.
2. C. A. L. Lamar to Gov. J. E. Brown, Feb. 23, 1861, C. A. L. Lamar Papers; *Official Records of the Union and Confederate Navies in the War of the Rebellion* (Washington, 1894-97), Ser. 2, I, 358.
3. *Ibid.,* Ser. 1, IV, 257.
4. *Ibid.,* Ser. 2, I, 235; Ser. 1, XVI, 591; XVII, 395, 416.
5. *Ibid.,* Ser. 1, XVI, 797-800.
6. *Ibid.,* Ser. 2, I, 235.
7. *Ibid.*
8. *Savannah Daily Morning News,* Nov. 24, 1865.
9. Winfield M. Thompson, "The Slave Yacht Wanderer," *Rudder,* XV (Feb.-April 1904), 242.
10. *G. B. Lamar, Sen., to Ex President Andrew Johnson* (n. p., ca. 1869).
11. Thompson, "The Slave Yacht Wanderer," p. 243.
12. Charles J. Montgomery, "Survivors from the Cargo of the Negro Slave Yacht Wanderer," *American Anthropologist,* I (Oct. 1906); Margaret Davis Cates, *Our Todays and Yesterdays* (Brunswick, Georgia, 1930); MS interviews, Manuscript Collection, University of Georgia.
13. There is an extensive file on this subject in Register of Letters Received by Secretary of Interior, National Archives (Microcopy 160, Rolls 1, 2, and 6).

Bibliography

Material on the *Wanderer* is scattered; the search for information was more a case of finding pieces of a jigsaw puzzle than of dusting off and repairing a painting. The few articles in periodicals and the references in books were fragmentary, incomplete, and often misleading. No single group of letters or diaries gave a coherent story.

Manuscripts

The National Archives contains much material on the illicit African slave trade in general, and some on the *Wanderer* in particular. The main source is in the records of the office of the Secretary of the Interior relating to the suppression of the African slave trade and Negro colonization (Record Group 48). A large part of this record group, which includes much African squadron material, is on microfilm (Microcopy 160). Information on ship characteristics, ownership, and disposal is found in the Records of Registry and Records of Enrollment in the Treasury Department archives, as are letters between the Solicitor of the Treasury and the United States marshals. The Justice Department section contains instructions to United States attorneys and their reports to the attorney general. State Department archives have much on slavers in general but little about the *Wanderer*. Navy Department records (Record Group 45) include letters to and from commanding officers of ships, and logs of the ships. Although the *Wanderer* did not loom large in these records, there are numerous comments about her.

Copies of documents such as pages of ships' logs and Admiralty correspondence with Admiral Grey were furnished by the Public Record Office, London. These items refute the widely held view that the *Wanderer's* true character was unknown to the British.

The Library of Congress has a *Wanderer* file which contains some notes of Hamilton Couper, the shipping papers for the *Wanderer's* crew, and miscellaneous papers on the subject, as well as some of the verbatim testimony in the trials of Brown, Rajesta, and Arguivi.

The Federal Records Center at East Point, Georgia, has the records of the United States and Confederate States courts for the Georgia district and circuit courts.

The Georgia Department of Archives and History contains information about Charles Lamar. Since the *Wanderer* cases were federal, the *Wanderer* does not appear in Georgia or Chatham County records.

A log of the *Wanderer* is in the Special Collections, Emory University Library. Mrs. Albert Howell of Atlanta, a great granddaughter of Charles Lamar, has deposited a number of Lamar's vivid and frank letters to his father and others in the same library. A collection of material on Carey W. Styles includes an inaccurate account of the *Wanderer* episode written by Styles's daughter many years after the event, and is also at Emory.

The Georgia Collection of the University of Georgia has useful and interesting items on the *Wanderer* and the Lamar family. Gazaway B. Lamar's letters and ledgers give some insight into the affairs of that busy man. The large Howell Cobb collection has some useful letters, including two from Henry Jackson about the *Wanderer* trials, and some comments on Charles Lamar's slave dealings by Mary Ann Cobb and John B. Lamar.

Two collections at Duke University were of use: the Godfrey Barnsley letters gave slight background information on Savannah society and Charles Lamar. The diary of Lt. J. W. Jones, U. S. Navy, gave a graphic picture of the operations of the African squadron, 1859-1860.

William Porcher Mile's correspondence with William Henry Trescot held by the University of North Carolina contains an interesting exchange of opinion of highly placed South Carolinians over Magrath's rulings in Corrie's case.

Pamphlets

Henry R. Jackson's pamphlet *The Wanderer Case; the Speech of Hon. Henry R. Jackson of Savannah, Ga.* (Atlanta, ca. 1891), although written many years after the events it describes, gives a good idea of Jackson's attitude. Likewise, Charles A. L. Lamar's pamphlet *The Reply of C. A. L. Lamar of Savannah, Georgia, to the Letter of Hon. Howell Cobb, Secretary of the Treasury of the United States, Refusing a Clearance to the Ship Richard Cobden* (Charleston, 1858) is a forthright statement of Charles Lamar's principles. Gazaway B. Lamar's *G. B. Lamar, Sen., to Ex President Andrew Johnson* (n. p. ca. 1869) sheds some light on the *Wanderer's* disposition after Martin's venture. The first of these pamphlets is widely available; the latter two are in the Georgia Collection at the University of Georgia. A fourth pamphlet, *United States of America by Information versus the Schooner Wanderer and Cargo* (n. p., n. d., ca. 1860) containing verbatim testimony of the *Wanderer's* trial is among Caleb Cushing Papers in the Library of Congress.

Periodicals

By all odds, the anonymous "A Slave-Trader's Letter-Book," *North American Review,* CXLIII (1886), was the most useful article read. I have no doubt of the authenticity of these letters; they agree in style with

Lamar's writing and in detail with material from other contemporary sources, including family letters retained by the Lamar family more than a hundred years. The editing is poor, many letters are cut, but the substance has been preserved.

The *Rudder,* XV (February-April, 1904), has a series of articles entitled "The Slave Yacht Wanderer" by Winfield M. Thompson. These articles are inaccurate in some minor details but are the best account published to date. They have excellent information on the design and construction of the yacht and on her career after the Civil War. The *American Anthropologist,* I (October, 1906), includes the article "Survivors from the Cargo of the Negro Slave Yacht Wanderer" by Charles J. Montgomery. In many ways disappointing (nothing is told about loading, transporting, or landing the slaves), this article is understandably preoccupied with language, handcraft, and superstitions of the interviewed survivors but also shows where some of the Negroes lived their lives. F. B. C. Bradlee's "Last of the American Slavers," *Marine Journal,* May 22, 1926, is an unreliable rehash of erroneous information from the Spears account discussed in the book section of this bibliography.

Two articles by Laura A. White, "The South in the 1850's As Seen by British Consuls," *Journal of Southern History,* I (1933), and "The United States in the 1850's As Seen by British Consuls," *Mississippi Valley Historical Review,* XIX (1933), contain the information and attitudes of the British consular officials on the *Wanderer* episode. Harvey Wish's "The Revival of the African Slave Trade in the United States, 1856-1860," *Mississippi Valley Historical Review,* XXVIII (1941), is a first-rate piece of historical writing. It is concerned with the efforts of Leonidas W. Spratt to legalize the trade, but it has an accurate and concise treatment of the *Wanderer.*

There have been several articles of importance to this study in the *Georgia Historical Quarterly.* Warren Grice's "The Confederate States Court," IX (1925), deals principally with Martin's trials. Three articles about the Lamar family were of interest as background material. Alexander Crosby Brown's "The John Randolph: America's First Commercially Successful Iron Steamboat," XXXVI (1952), tells of Gazaway B. Lamar's early enterprise. Thomas Robson Hay's "Gazaway Bugg Lamar, Confederate Banker and Business Man," XXXVII (1953), has a good short account of the *Wanderer* incident. Gazaway Lamar's sister Mrs. Hugh McLeod (Rebecca Lamar) wrote an account of her harrowing experience in "The Loss of the Steamer *Pulaski,*" III (1919).

Newspapers

The most valuable newspaper was the *Savannah Daily Morning News* which gave much space to detailed accounts of testimony during the *Wanderer* trials. Although only a few numbers of the *Savannah Republican* are in existence, it was regularly quoted in the *New York Herald, New York Times,* and *Washington National Intelligencer.* The latter three papers gave wide and detailed coverage to all the doings of the *Wanderer* and the men connected with her. Garrison's *Liberator* had nothing of value. The *Charleston Courier* and those issues of the *Charleston Mercury* available gave good coverage of happenings in Magrath's court. The *Spirit of the Times* added bits of information on the *Wanderer's* sporting career. The *New York Tribune,* although it gave comparatively light coverage of the *Wanderer* as a slaver, did supply Charles Lamar's captured Civil War correspondence. The *Southern Argus* (Norfolk) and *Augusta Daily Constitutionalist* contributed bits and pieces, particularly on the distribution of the *Wanderer's* slaves.

Government Documents and Public Correspondence

Richard Peters (ed.), *The Public Statutes at Large of the United States of America* (Boston, 1854) and William M. Malloy (comp.), *Treaties, Conventions, International Acts, Protocols and Agreements between the United States of America and other Powers, 1776-1909* (Washington, 1910) furnished reliable copies of the materials which their titles indicate. The two great official works on the Civil War operations, *The War of the Rebellion: A Compilation of the Official Records of the Union and Confederate Armies* (Washington, 1880-1901) and *Official Record of the Union and Confederate Navies in the War of the Rebellion* (Washington, 1894-1927), as well as Allen D. Candler (ed.), *The Confederate Records of the State of Georgia* (Atlanta, 1909), were useful in tracing the Civil War careers of the yacht *Wanderer* and of some of the men who had been involved with her. Reports of the Secretary of the Navy for 1858-1861 gave a good picture of the problem of capturing slavers as did *Senate Executive Document 49, 35th Congress, 1st Session* and *House Executive Document I, 36th Congress, 2nd Session. The Federal Cases, Comprising Cases Argued and Determined in the Circuit and District Courts of the United States* (St. Paul, 1894-97) gives brief summaries of the evidence and law in the *Wanderer* cases and verbatim opinions, substantiating the detailed reports contained in the newspapers mentioned.

Books

There is no book-length account of the *Wanderer's* expedition. The most widely used material is that contained in John R. Spears, *The American Slave Trade* (New York, 1900). Unfortunately, the highly readable chapter on the *Wanderer* is based principally on the vague recollections of a Captain McGhee, made about forty years after the events. McGhee, who claimed to have been a shareholder in the slaving venture, remembered a voyage that could not have occurred, incidents that did not happen, and people who were not present. For instance, Spears writes that 750 slaves were taken on board in Africa, a figure clearly in error. He further quoted McGhee in a fanciful story of how the captain, whom he incorrectly identifies as a brother of Raphael Semmes of the *Alabama,* brought the *Wanderer* up the Savannah River at night. He says that Lamar gave a ball to which he invited officers and soldiers alike so that the

Wanderer could sneak past Fort Pulaski at night. The truth is that the *Wanderer* was seen by many witnesses at Jekyl Island and was brought up to Savannah by direction of law enforcement officers. A careful search of Savannah newspapers fails to disclose any grand ball to have been held during this period, and in 1858 Fort Pulaski had no garrison.

McGhee recounts a second slaving voyage to Africa for the *Wanderer* before she was stolen by Martin in October, 1859. She is said to have grounded between Jekyll and Cumberland islands in December and to have drowned a number of her slave cargo. This voyage could not have happened; the *Wanderer* was never out of port for more than a few days in that entire year. McGhee then says that the *Wanderer* was blockaded in the Savannah River in 1860 and finally was sold to the Confederate government. She was not blockaded in the Savannah River and was never owned or operated under the Confederacy. That an old man like McGhee, who might indeed have been part owner of the *Wanderer* in 1858, should have become confused in an interview half-century later is no surprise.

The Spears story is followed in the preface of George S. King's *The Last Slaver* (New York, 1933), Christopher Lloyd, *The Navy and the Slave Trade* (London, 1929), and George Francis Dow, *Slave Ships and Slaving* (Salem, Mass., 1927).

Warren S. Howard, *American Slavers and the Federal Law, 1837-1862* (Berkeley and Los Angeles, 1963) is a first-rate, highly readable, and reliable book. Howard believes "A Slave-Trader's Letter-book" to be a hoax. An earlier work is William E. B. Dubois, *The Suppression of the African Slave Trade to the United States of America* (New York, 1894). Although Dubois was a master at assembling data to support a preconceived idea (in this case, that the South was united in favoring the continued importation of African Negroes) he assembled an excellent bibliography of government documents and a good chronology. Hugh G. Soulsby, *The Right of Search and the Slave Trade in Anglo-American Relations, 1814-1862* (Baltimore, 1933) is a good account of the diplomatic problems of the United States' African squadron. Lloyd's book, cited above, and William Law Mathieson, *Great Britain and the Slave Trade* (London, 1929) give good pictures of the British efforts.

The best account of the *Wanderer* trials is in Alexander A. Lawrence, *James Moore Wayne, Southern Unionist* (Chapel Hill, 1943). William M. Robinson, Jr., *Justice in Grey* (Cambridge, 1941) and Rembert W. Patrick (ed.), *Opinions of the Confederate Attorneys General, 1861-1865* (Buffalo, 1950), are both good on Martin's trial for theft of the *Wanderer*.

Sarah A. Wallace and Frances E. Gillespie (eds.), *The Journal of Benjamin Moran, 1857-65* (Chicago, 1948), contains information on Captain Martin after the *Wanderer* abandoned him at sea.

For general information on coastal Georgia, Margaret Davis Cate, *Our Todays and Yesterdays* (Brunswick, Ga., 1930) and Burnette Vanstory, *Georgia's Land of the Golden Isles* (Athens, 1956) were useful.

Index

CPSIA information can be obtained
at www.ICGtesting.com
Printed in the USA
LVHW040510150223
739566LV00001B/171